The Search for Purpose and Meanings: In Life and From Death

Sohan Singh

D K's BOOKS FOR ALL
Delhi-110052

First Published 2010

ISBN 13: 978-81-7386-282-6
ISBN 10: 81-7386-282-3

Published By
DK's BOOKS FOR ALL
(an imprint of Low Price Publications)
A-6, Second Floor, Nimri Commercial Centre,
Ashok Vihar Phase-4, Delhi - 110 052
Tel.: +91 11 2730 2453
website: www.Lppindia.com
e-mail: info@Lppindia.com

Printed At
D K Fine Art Press P Ltd.
Delhi-110052

PRINTED IN INDIA

To All humanity

All mankind is one, though misgivings are many.

(Guru Granth Sahib)

Acknowledgements

I have Peter Davidson and Mike Atkinson to thank the most. They edited the book and gave me invaluable advice and numerous suggestions. They were both very encouraging and kept me on the ball.

I am very grateful to Malik Chaudhry and Throssel Hole Buddhist Abbey for agreeing to be interviewed and spending considerable time with this author. They enlightened me on Islam and Buddhism.

I must express my gratitude to Reverend Diana MacNaughton, Charles Slater, Acharya Krishan K.Attri and Dr Anand for going through material on Christianity, Judaism and Hinduism respectively.

I am indebted to scholars and writers whose works have enabled me to stay focused. The list of references at the end partially records that debt.

Many thanks also go to Ahmad Khoshnoudi for designing the book cover.

I am also grateful to my family for their understanding and patience.

Contents

Foreword

In this his third book, Sohan Singh turns his penetrative gaze on that great inevitability, death. As the saying goes, there are only two certainties in life, the other one being taxes. Indeed, this is Sohan's theme throughout. He is at pains to emphasis that since death is unavoidable we should all take time to consider how we are going to cope with it.

As death will summon us one day, the reader is encouraged to have a sense of meaning and purpose in life. People who lead meaningful lives feel good when they think of what they have done in the past and hope to do in the future. They have a sense of direction. The awareness or recognition that no material possession will accompany us to the next world helps us to be more mindful of our deeds or karma. One who is mindful of these factors will only do those deeds or karma which are helpful to humankind.

On several occasions he points out how we appear so afraid of the subject that we avoid discussing it at all costs. Again and again he criticises the way in which we all endeavour to talk about everything but this all important issue. But since each and every one of us must face it eventually, it is vital that we bite the bullet. Sooner or later we all have to think about the future, a future where our existence on this planet will come to an end.

Some day we are all going to kick the bucket, shuffle off this mortal coil; go to meet our maker; be pushing up daisies; be six foot under or be measured for an oblong box. We are all going to snuff it; conk out; breathe our last breath or be heaven bound. We are all going to peg it; pass away; pass over or get to life's end.

It's quite incredible the number of euphemisms we have for it. The humour in the above indicates one way in which we deal with it. Death is but the start of a long journey. However, it's a journey into the unknown. Perhaps this is what we fear—not the fact itself—but the truth that we cannot be sure what comes next.

Sohan devotes an entire chapter to as many of the propositions put forward concerning what comes after death. He has been quite thorough when considering the views of all the great sages. I found this exercise extremely enlightening and believe has done as much as he could to cover these views. I did not take the book lightly. Having read it, I have questioned Sohan at length about everything he has included and added some comments of my own. So I can say without any hesitation that he has made a serious attempt to provide some valuable positive ideas. The ideas he has incorporated with a view to assisting us in coming to terms with our inevitable end, I believe will help us to cope with the difficult issue.

Some of my comments concerned the concept of karma. It is my view that this notion saves us a lot of time. I say this because if we are trying to lessen our karmic retribution then this can only be achieved if we act in the best possible ways. These would be ways which are the most beneficial for all. Similarly I argue that if we believe in a law of cause and effect we do not need moral codes, the mere wish to make the best possible causes would prevent us from actions which were detrimental to others. I put these points to Sohan and I am sure he has reflected on them before finalising this book.

For my part, I believe that this useful read will provide each of us with a reference source. It is full of wisdom and positive thinking on a very tricky issue. It can provide reassurance when we lose a loved one. Sohan further covers the process of grief in a sensitive and mature way. I believe that everyone who reads it will benefit from it.

Peter. W. Davidson BA (Hons), Dip HE
Trustee, National Association of Writers Groups (UK)

Introduction

Some of the most asked and discussed questions in serious discourses in every culture, and country are: Is there a meaning in life? Does the universe have a purpose? What really exists and what does 'existence' mean? Does death have a purpose, or is it just the cessation of life? Do human beings have free will to change, to think and act differently or do we have conditioned minds, which is the result of our past history as well as the cultural influences we inherited? Is there a God? If there is God why does He / She or It allow destruction and catastrophes?

This book is based on the firm belief that we have a purpose and a meaning to life and an ability to accept death when our tenure on this planet comes to an end. It endeavours to consider the fundamental questions of life and death, of purpose and meanings. It also looks at futility and meaninglessness of some thought processes and subsequent behaviour.

Just as an artist works with forms and colours, and a novelist works with plots, characters and actions, so I have looked at ideas , concepts and questions advanced by principal religions, philosophers and psychologists to sculpture or shape a view. I have examined various religious beliefs which have influenced the world, and studied the works of different philosophers. Just like there are many different religions, there are several branches of philosophy also. Some are difficult to comprehend, so an attempt has been made to get to grips with the synthesis of different ideas and insights, to analyse them and to present them in a clear and succinct manner.

I have frequently quoted the words of Prophets, Messengers or Gurus like Buddha, Jesus Christ, Krishna, Muhammad, Mahavira, Guru Nanak and Guru Gobind singh. They have not been quoted in order to compare, but because of a profound respect for them and their beliefs. They have a lot to teach us. Their writings and pronouncements come in many forms, but have lot of commonality essential for our spiritual advancement. Some of these forms, no doubt have become overlaid with extraneous matters, misrepresentations and distortions, that their *essence* has been obscured by them. Therefore, up to a large extent their deeper meaning is no longer recognised, and their transformative power is reduced if not lost. I have quoted their thoughts, to reveal their deeper meaning and relevance to us today.

This book is also my journey to find if life can be more meaningful, and to use the fear of death to advantage. Somebody accidentally threw me into a red hot oven or hearth designed for parching grain when I was about six years old. My cousin brother pulled me out. I am told that if I had stayed there for another six or seven seconds more, I would have been ashes. I still bear the scars. Then in my youth, I slipped when descending Mt Kenya, and rolled like a rag doll for about a hundred yards. A huge rock stopped my rapid descent. Experienced mountain guides and mountaineers said that they have rarely seen somebody survive such a fall.

We all have accidents, shocks and bereavements that force us to step back for sometime to reflect to seek real meaning and purpose to life, and if death has some unstated **meaning** or significance for us. After all death is the 'truth', it will visit us sooner or later, as life is transient. Benjamin Franklin believed that the two certainties in life are death and taxes.

Perhaps the death of a close relative of mine prompted deep reflection. I was a participant observer which probably sowed the seeds of this 'work.' She had been terminally ill for a long time, and we were relieved that she had passed to the next world rather than lingering in pain. Her death made me very conscious of my mortality, and that we all are susceptible to a terminal or chronic illness. We cannot regulate when we die, and we do not live in some science fiction depictions where the state can decide. Humans have free will, but are bound by the laws of nature. While living on this mother earth, we can think and decide if there is more to life than we imagine, and search for meaning in our daily lives that can be religious or spiritual.

This body and soul is not ours. It has been given to us on rent. The rent is to make our life as meaningful as possible. Sooner or later the landlord will ask us to vacate the property we occupy. It is right that contemplation of our mortality and suffering has been an essential part of human experience, and to many it seems not only arrogant but unrealistic to dismiss these questions out of hand. Those who have a belief in the Supreme Being would agree with Karen Armstrong when she says that, 'God may be incomprehensible, but people have the option of putting their trust in this ineffable God and affirming a meaning, even in the midst of meaninglessness.'

Writing this book has compelled me to look within myself, to explore deeper and deeper, to search for answers which are difficult to find if we are focused on external matters only. Most of the time, I speak from inner experience, the true source within, which does not lie to you. I do not claim to tell you any new spiritual truth, or provide another meaning or purpose to life that deep within you don't know already. All that I have done is to bring out that which we have not cared to refresh, or develop and hence is forgotten or ignored.

Chapter 1

Can Death Provide a Meaning for Life?

O eloquent, just, and mighty Death!....though hast drawn together all the far stretched greatness, all the pride, cruelty, and ambition of man, and covered it all over with these two narrow words, *Hic jacet* (Here lies).

(The History of the world) (1614)

'To find freedom in this life, one has to come to terms with death. We have to contemplate the end of our existence as we know it, and our fears that surround it.' (D. Morgan). To face death is to face the unknown, as in our consciousness, death is never possible.

In western society, people generally avoid a conversation about death even when it lurks around the corner. People from the Indian sub continent will talk about it indirectly, in terms of life after death and what can be done to avoid transmigration or going to heaven or hell. Such a discussion normally takes place only when somebody has done a good deed, like giving large sums of money to a charity or in religious discourses. Death is the only inevitably we face, and it is a curious flaw in our characters that we should avoid discussing or thinking about something we know for sure is going to happen. It does not make death any less painful or easier. If anything, the opposite is true.

Buddhism has flowed into countless different forms of expression, but its understanding of death begins with the early experiences of Gautama. He became known as Buddha (the Enlightened One) when he saw the entire truth of all things. Gautama was born a prince and his father in the palace protected him from any sight which might be disturbing or threatening.

But then one day, Gautama ordered his carriage driver to take him out in the countryside, and he saw a sick person for the first time. Gautama found the experience disturbing. On his second drive, he saw an old person and on the third occasion a dead body prepared for cremation. Gautama was seeking some remedy or way of dealing with disease and death when he went out the fourth time. On this drive, he saw a sadhu or an ascetic wearing saffron robes. There are loads of fake sadhus in India today, but the genuine ascetics practise detachment from all worldly entanglements in this life. Gautama understood that he would experience the same things too sooner or later. These realizations lead him to leave the palace as quickly as he could. He abandoned his wife and son, Rahula and threw himself into the practice of austerity and detachment.

Later in life, Gautama went onto even more extreme practices, in his attempt to discern some absolute reality in himself which would not be touched by the process of decay and death. In the end, he realized that none of these practices could rescue him from death. On attaining his Enlightenment, or complete transcendence, Buddha came to the realization that there is nothing—no thing –which is not subject to transience (anicca), change and dissolution.

Even though death is a natural part of life, we find it difficult to perceive our own death, and up to a certain extent believe in our immortality. We can only perceive other people's death. We hear news of numbers of people killed in battle, by disease, by malnutrition in Asia and Africa, but they are seen as distant places.

The reality is that with the rapid technical advances and scientific achievements, nations have been able to develop weapons of mass destruction which increase the fear of a violent and probably sudden death. We live in frightening times. As human beings, if we start from scratch to attempt to conceive our own death, then we can learn to face what is inevitable with more rationality and less fear. Death is something that hardly any body aspires to, but the very fact that we are born, means that it is unavoidable.

Nowadays even doctors or medical practitioners feel uncomfortable when talking about death. They talk about prolonging life at any cost and rarely about death being unavoidable. Old doctors who grew up a generation ago in an environment which used few defence mechanisms or euphemisms and faced death as a reality.

In the past generations, death in infancy and early childhood was frequent, and there were few who didn't lose a member of the family at an early age. May be instead of thinking about prolonging life at all costs, and increasing the suffering of the patient, we should aim to develop ourselves to be able to cope with death better. We should not shun from a dialogue on the topic to help people to live less fearfully of what is after all inevitable.

Patients who are very sick, or who have been unwell over a long period, sometimes welcome the end of their lives. They want to end their suffering. Sometimes there are discussions about euthanasia and assisted death, and people are much divided about such issues. My own father, who had throat cancer, wanted me to ask the doctor to end his life by way of a lethal injection. It was painful for me to realise that his suffering was intolerable for him, but I couldn't go along with his wishes because of my belief in sanctity of life.

Death is a natural part of life, a part which we will all surely have to face sooner or later. Some of us tend to ignore it, the fact is, whether we choose to ignore it, or face it, we cannot escape it.

If we can confront the prospect of our death, and by meditating on it, try to minimize the suffering that it can bring. If we contemplate the possibility of our end, we may wish to change many things, perhaps think more about the welfare of our families, nation, and humanity as a whole.

The fact is that our life on this earth decreases every day, it is getting smaller every second. So when some body celebrates a birthday, the person's life has decreased by one year. Our business may be expanding, our family may be growing bigger, but we are not getting any younger.

When a dear one is dying, all the arguments you have had, appear unimportant or meaningless. Around death, things which were seen as profound suddenly appear trivial. Fragmented families might wish to resolve their differences by facing and accepting the reality of death. Quarrels and differences which seem intractable and wide ranging, may appear to be petty and of no consequence when seen in a different light. Deep reflection can help us to make sense of our life which may lead to a change for the better or to decide to adopt a more ethical lifestyle for ourselves. Exhortations to lead a good life often go unheeded, but things tend to change when one develops an insight into suffering and the impermanence of our lives.

By constantly reminding ourselves of our temporary stay on this earth, we may achieve peace. It could be our own peace of mind as desires would be fewer; people will not be driven by passions and battered by disappointments. Those who want to change the world for the better would find it easier to try to bring an end to internal and international conflicts.

Naturally most of us would like to die a peaceful and 'natural' death, but it is not really possible to achieve equanimity in life and a quiet departure from this world if we are leading a violent life style, or our minds are agitated by emotions like lust, anger craving, and fear. To achieve this type of death, we should try to cultivate inner peace and overcome our negativity.

Contemplation of death, may lead to some profound and beneficial experiences. It is only when we think deeply about our mortality, that we become seriously concerned about purpose and meaning in life. Death shows how little time we have on this earth. If you talk to people when they have lost a dear one, they will tell you that around death, 'all things seem trivial or of no great significance.' With some the feeling disappears after a few minutes, or after the funeral, but with others, it can linger for a long time. Such people who reflect on life and death, think about what is 'good to do,' and try to find a new basis for life.

Human life has been likened to the shadow of a tree in Guru Granth Sahib (Holy Scripture of the Sikhs). 'Who ever attaches to a shadow of the tree, repents when the shadow which is temporary passes off. What ever is visible must pass away.' I hope some ideas expressed in this work will relieve some of the suffering and fear of death that so many of us undergo.

After Life

Death and life are not far apart. When I look for their origin it goes back into infinity; when I look for their end, it proceeds without termination. Life is the follower of death and death is the predecessor of life. (Chuang Tzu)

'Afterlife denotes supposed existence in some spiritual or mental form after bodily death.' However if there is one question that could truly be said to concern us all, it is the enduring mystery of life after death. We all wonder as to what happens when we die and what—if anything awaits us when we have crossed the 'final frontier.'

Though atheists like Richard Dawkins would not agree, but most of the great traditions of the world tell us that death is not the end, at least not of the soul. But despite their teachings people in this age imagine that the life as we have now is all there is. With such an attitude, it is difficult to infuse this life that we are leading with any **sacred meaning**. Without any real or authentic faith in an after life, most people live without any purpose or meaning. Our vision is limited to a few years, and does not go much beyond middle age.

The disastrous effects of the denial go far beyond the individual. They affect the planets as well. There is nothing to restrain us from plundering the mother earth for our individual needs. Our selfish lifestyle is already proving fatal for the future. Global warning is already having an impact and some activists talk of leaving very little or nothing to our children or grand children. Some scientists contend that it is not too late to reverse the damage, and activists who expect the worst are short-sighted. Lately, most of the governments have started taking the issue seriously, but whether their resolve to limit the damage bears fruit remains to be seen.

As there is little belief in life after this one, we have created a society fixated on quick gains, without any regard for the consequences of our actions. It could be the major reason why we have a world in which individuality is paramount, and we are living for immediate gratification, without compassion or regard for the welfare of the others.

Our society is obsessed with fame and has more interest in what is happening to celebrities than saving the planet. Celebrities are our icons, the new gods and we spend so much time following what ever they do, that we have no time to focus on serious issues like climate change and global warning. Al Gore the Nobel Prize winner said at the UN Climate Change Conference in Poland: "It's wrong for this generation to destroy the habitability of the planet and ruin the prospects of every generation." The star of the Oscar winning film, *An Inconvenient Truth* called for global targets to cut carbon emissions to be toughened to take account of new scientific evidence that claims the world is warming faster than expected. He said the celebrity obsessed world had lost its way, and added: "We have to overcome the paralysis that has prevented us from acting and focus clearly and unblinkingly on this crisis rather than spending so much time on OJ Simpson and other celebrities.

Making Sense of Life and Death

'Most of the people are caught in the whirlpool of worldly pleasure and have lost the real meaning of living a life.'

'It's only when we truly know and understand that we have a limited time on earth—and we have no way of knowing when that time is up—that we will begin to live each day to the fullest as if it was the only one we had.'

(Dr. Elizabeth Kubler-Ross.)

Why are we so afraid of death? Is it because we have not understood the law of nature? Death is all around us in nature. Our forefathers had a realistic view of death; they saw it happen very often in their lives and believed that it would happen to them sooner or later. Since the breath returns to the air, and the body to the dust, there is nothing that can survive. 'He is fully confident in his mind that he is immortal and the thought of death never comes to his mind' (Guru Granth Sahib). People push death to the edge of their lives, as they push the knowledge of their own mortality to the farthest extremes of their consciousness.

We have heard of suicides, cancer, motor neuron disease, accidents, and wars finishing the lives of so many young and vibrant people. Old age sickness and decay have snuffed the life out of many elderly people who wanted a lot more living to do. We do not believe the reality, we are obsessed with prolonging our life and do not want to confront death. Terminally ill patients normally know that they have little time left on this earth and may want to make the necessary arrangements before their departure. When somebody is on a death bed, or death's door, we give false comforts: 'You will be alright soon, you are too young to die' are the common statements made to cheer up those who tell us that they believe that their end is approaching.

Our love of life and fear of death mean that we seldom prepare either for death itself or for the process of dying. We cannot prepare for it because we do not want to think about it. Intellectually we know that death will come to us one day, but always believe that it is far away. If we do not accept our true nature, and not come to terms with our impermanence on this planet, death can be very frightening. Death is frightening, and the fear of death is a universal fear.

It is only when we are able to come face to face with our own direst fears and vulnerability that we can step into the unknown with courage. Fear of death is the same as fear of life. When we feel deeply, and truly know the experience, we can let it pass by and gain our tranquillity.

A German photographer held an exhibition in London in June 2008. This profound little exhibition was of photographs taken of people before and immediately after they died. Walter Schols who was terrified of death wanted to confront it through his art just like I am trying to come to terms with it through this work. The words alongside the portraits reflected the anger, fear, courage or resignation his sitters felt at the imminence of their death.

If we could only follow Elizabeth Kubler- Ross's advice: "If all of us would make an all out effort to contemplate our death, to deal with our anxieties surrounding the concept of death, and to help others familiarize themselves with these thoughts, perhaps we would find it easier to accept our mortality, and those of others close to us. If we cannot deny death, we need to learn to accept it gracefully"

"Death has never been really accepted in any culture, it is distasteful, though we all know deep down in our hearts that it is inevitable". (Elizabeth Kubler- Ross). Advances in technology and science in the last decades are ultimately responsible for the increased fear of death and the rising number of emotional problems. We are told that if you use this prescribed drug and that medicine, you can expect to live up to 85 or 95. Medicine in general is more geared to prolonging life rather than diminishing human suffering.

Physicians have more people in their waiting rooms with their emotional problems than they have ever had before, but they also have more elderly patients who not only try to live with their decreased physical abilities and limitations but who also face loneliness and isolation with all its pains and anguish.

Dr. William says over anxious and over acquisitive ways are symptoms of our own reluctance to ponder the awful fact of our mortality. Guru Gobind Singh (the tenth spiritual teacher of the Sikhs) accentuates the inevitability of death thus: "If some emperors possess tall incomparable elephants painted in bright colours, adorned with golden trapping. (You can substitute cars for elephants). If they were to own millions of horses, capable of fleeting at a speed greater than wind and bounding like deer. What matters if such powerful emperors exist (or existed)? Because they depart bare-footed in the end (to the next world)."

'Never has it been easier than now to avoid thinking about our demise. Our grandparents knew a world in which women died at childbirth, brothers and sisters were buried in infancy, soldiers and civilians were frequent casualties of war. But better child care and universal education has ensured low mortality among children. The many diseases that took a big toll among the young and middle aged have been conquered especially in the advanced countries.'

Advancement in science and technology have greatly benefitted humankind but not without a price. Without any doubt, they have improved our quality of our life, we have machines and medicines to cure us or reduce and eradicate diseases. If we have motor vehicles to transport us to any place we wish to go, there are armoured vehicles, tanks and fighter planes to kill others also. Destructive weapons have been created, and people all over the world live in fear of a terrorist attack or a nuclear war breaking out. Despite attempts to reduce numbers of weapons, thousands upon thousands of nuclear weapons are poised for attack and countries which do not have them are endeavouring to acquire them. Some countries celebrate their national events by way of military parades where the latest tanks, aeroplanes and nuclear missiles are shown off.

Let us take another example regarding the damage and destruction a weapon can wreak. Writer Roberto Saviano in an article entitled, 'The World's Deadliest Weapon' says that, nothing in the world—organic or synthetic, metal or chemical—has produced more deaths than AK-47 rifle. It has killed more than the atom bombs dropped on Hiroshima and Nagasaki, more than HIV, more than the bubonic plague, more than malaria, more than all the attacks by Islamic fundamentalists, more than all the earthquakes in history.

Massacres perpetrated with AK-47 –verified by the United Nations, have taken place in countries including Algeria, Uganda and Haiti. More than 50 regular armies use AK-47 and statistics on the irregular paramilitary and guerrilla groups that use them are difficult to calculate. Approximately 150 million Kalashnikovs rifles of varying models have been produced all based on General Mikhail Kalashnikov's original design.

Human life is a small matter in cosmic terms, and its cycle of life. We need to see our own death in cosmic terms, natural and nothing to be afraid of if it is measured against the great scheme of things. If we rationally base our beliefs on what we know to be inevitable, we will suffer neither fear nor anguish. *There is no cure for birth and death, save to enjoy the interval.* (George Santayana)

Immortality

A scientist by the name of Aubrey de Grey says that one day we will eventually be able to live till we are 1,000. Aubrey de Grey thinks that we will be able to restore our youth so that we will always be in our prime! Even though life is short at present, it is not uncommon to hear of people getting bored, or having nothing to do after retirement. I wonder how many people would like to live for ever. How do you feel alive when you know that you are never going to die? If we lived for such a long time, we had get bored of our immortality. Can you imagine the population if people lived for ten centuries?

Death is a necessity in that it helps to maintain the balance on this planet.

Shiva—(The third god of the Hindu triad)

The three main Hindu gods are: Brahma, the creator, Vishnu, the preserver, Shiva, the destroyer. It is said that Shiva used to go around with snakes around his neck and ashes on his body. The snakes used to move around his neck like a rosary or prayer beads and symbolized death. In other words, snakes could strike anytime and end his life. The ashes were meant to tell people that after cremation their body will turn to ashes (or to dust if the body is buried). Shiva, instead of giving long sermons had a quick and practical way of showing our impermanence on this planet. The snakes signified death, and ashes illustrated what happens to the body (corpse) after death

Similarly the Sword of Damocles has a similar message. In classical legend Damocles lived in 4th century BC, and was a courtier of the Greek ruler Dionysius 1. When Damocles made too much of his sovereign's good fortune, Dionysius invited Damocles to a feast. The king symbolically hung a sword over Damocles' head suspended by a single hair to demonstrate the precariousness of happiness.

Socrates' Views On Death

I am confident that there truly is such a thing as living again, that the living spring from the dead, and that the souls of the dead are in existence. (Socrates)

In Athens in 399 BC, Socrates was tried, found guilty and condemned to death 'for encouraging young people to think.' The 70 year old philosopher made a speech in his own defence and elucidated what death meant to him. His view was that there is a great hope that death is a blessing For him to die is one of two things, the dead may be annihilated and have no sensations of anything whatever, or there is a certain change and passage of the soul from one place to another. If it is a privation of all sensations, as it were a sleep in which the sleeper has no dream, death would be a wonderful gain. It is a gain, for thus the future appears to be nothing more than one night.

On the other hand, if death is a removal from here to another place, and what is said is true, that all the dead are there, then he couldn't ask for a greater blessing from the judges who had condemned him to death. For in Hades, he shall find those who are true judges, and would be released from those who pretend to be judges. He wondered if it would be a sad removal as he would find demigods who were just in their own life. Socrates couldn't fix a prize on a conference with philosophers like Orpheus, and Homer. His greatest pleasure would be to spend his time questioning and examining the people in Hades as he had done on the earth discovering who amongst them is wise and who fancies himself to be wise but is not.

Socrates indicated to the judges that they ought to entertain good hopes with respect to death, and to meditate on the one truth, that to a good man nothing is evil, neither while living nor when dead. His concerns are not neglected by the gods. Socrates concluded his speech with the following words: "But now is the time to depart—for me to die and for you to live. But which of us is going to a better state is unknown to anyone but God.

Other Philosophers' Views

The coward dies many times before his death. (Shakespeare).

To make ourselves strong and secure from harm, said Epicurus, we need to get a clear understanding of four matters, God, death, pleasure and suffering. "All our fears and desires are comprehended in these four subjects, so to grasp the truth about them will free us and give peace of mind."

"If there is a deity, it is a blessed one and a tranquil being, not concerned with the burden of administering the world—for the world governs itself according to nature.

A deity is not actuated by anger or favour, nor possessed by any interest in imposing requirements of any kind on us. From such a being, we have nothing to fear. We can instead treat the idea of such a deity as a model for us to emulate, its peacefulness, detachment, and unending pleasure are exactly what we should seek to achieve in our lives.

Death happens at a definite time. It is the extinction of life. It is the dissolution of the physical elements we are made of, which return into the cosmos they came from. To fear the non-existence that ensues is as rational as to regret that we did not exist before we were conceived and born. (Believers in reincarnation though, feel sure that they had existed before their conception and their soul will live on. It is immortal.)

"Those who fear death perform an impossible feat, they imagine themselves witnessing their own non-existence and lamenting it. Superstitions and religious beliefs that tell of punishment in a post mortem state make people afraid of dying, but as soon as we see that death is simply an end, all such fear evaporates and once again we are free."

Aurelius' view of death is that human life is a small matter in cosmic terms, and its cycles of life, change and death are inevitable, not to be afraid of, and indeed not very important as measured against the great schemes of things. If we rationally base our belief on what we know to be inevitable, we will suffer neither fear nor anguish.

Restraint

Our ancestors feared wild animals, but in modern times, people fear other people. This is because of the production of deadly weapons which can be fired from a distance. You do not see the enemy, so no lone feels the pain and fear of the 'other person.' Swords and spears were replaced by guns and tanks, and they were for killing other human beings and subjugating nations. And now we have nuclear weapons. There is fear that some nations may use nuclear weapons against others. Some rogue leaders are not responsible enough to control their urge to use them for destructive purposes. Iran has threatened Israel with complete annihilation. The race is so dire that people of North Korea live in abject poverty, are malnourished but the leaders want to possess nuclear weapons.

If we **all** contemplate death, the world leaders who make the final choice of war and peace between nations, perhaps would not declare war so easily. Some people think that war is glamorous, and others delude themselves that death will happen to their enemy only. They need to contemplate that their men and women, their own soldiers and sailors and air personnel can also die and come back in body bags. Deaths are inevitable in a theatre of war, and it is never one sided even when you are winning it.

We may achieve our inner tranquillity as well as peace between nations by facing and accepting the certainty of our own death. Hawks of the world would think of the Golden Rule, 'Never to impose on others what you would not choose for yourself'or put simply—' not do to others what you would not want done to you

It is an ethical reminder. The rule reminds us to think of the consequences of actions performed in the name of a state or a nation. The question the hawks would be considering before taking a hard line would be: What if it happened to me? What would I think/ feel if my country is attacked? Some powerful countries take the view that the small countries or nations less powerful cannot attack them. The Rule in such cases should be interpreted as, 'we shouldn't do to others what we wouldn't want done to us if we were in their position and had their desires (Stephen Law). So they will not be speaking from their position of strength and might, but putting themselves in the other nation state's position.

On a micro level, there would fewer intra-fights, disputes between families, neighbours and groups etc. People contemplating death will be aware of their own mortality, and thinking more about the purpose and meaning of life. Why indulge in wrongdoing if we are not going to live for long? Life is too short; do we really want to waste it on arguments and feuds? Baba Farid says: "The graveyard beckons you." (Guru Granth Sahib). So if you know that your journey to the graveyard or crematorium is not far off, your mind will be occupied by higher aims and ideals.

Elizabeth Kubler-Ross takes the view that we do not want to think about death and when death comes to a near and dear one, the ending is always attributed to some outside malicious intervention. Some people who strongly believed in God suddenly start saying that they have lost faith in God. It cannot be God's will and if it is, then God cannot be kind etc. But then others recognise their own mortality when somebody close to them passes away and their belief in God is strengthened.

The Supreme Being

From the outset, I would like to say that I definitely believe in God. I have come to believe that through many small and big instances in my life that it is not possible for us to always be in control, and that there is some larger power at work around us. You can choose to call it Nature, Supreme Being or God.

Most people believe in the existence of God and some question it. The tone of the public is quite often sceptical or dismissive when discussing religion or God. Cardinal Murphy O' Connor takes the view that atheists are becoming 'more vocal and aggressive.' But though faith leaders may be nervous of atheists, it is worth noting that British Humanist Society's slogan which was promoted on London buses in 2008-9 that 'There is probably no God', would suggest a certain lack of conviction in their own belief.

I have been fortunate to have grown up around people from different community faiths and visited different religious sites especially when I worked as a coordinator of 'Who Am I Project'. The Project aimed to acquaint school children with different faiths and cultures. It was a pleasure and enlightening to talk to people who represented their community faiths at these visits. I believe that few places exude the kind of peaceful energy that these religious centres do. At least whilst people are at their respective religious places, they express gratitude for the things they have and try to be 'good' in both their thought and deed. Most of us forget to be grateful when things are going right in life. I feel a bit sorry for atheists—particularly for not having anyone to thank for their good fortune. Gratitude is a natural human response. It seems a bit churlish to take for granted the many wonders of the world.

The ontological argument crops up many times in the history of philosophy. Desecrates used sceptical methods only to arrive at indubitable truth. His so called *'method of doubt'* was aimed at establishing certainties. He tried to doubt every thing, even to imagine that the obvious were false. Descartes applied the method of doubt, and subjected all his beliefs to the very strongest doubts he can muster. In effect, he applies doubt as a *filter*. Those beliefs that fail to pass through the filter are set aside. Only those that pass safely through—that prove immune even to the severest doubt—are to be retained. After having filtered his beliefs until he finds those that are indubitable, Descartes then proceeds to rebuild the concepts systematically, based upon these certainties.

As regards the existence of God, Descrates doubted all he could, but at last found his indubitable principle, the existence of the self,–'I am because I think.' It formed the basis to find the proof of the existence of God. In his third meditation—Of God that exists, he says: "I am a thing that thinks, that is to say that doubts, affirms, denies, that knows a few things, that is ignorant of many (that loves, that hates), that wills, that desires, that also imagines and perceives—.

Descartes understood God to be a substance that is infinite (eternal, immutable), independent, all knowing, all powerful, by which he and everything else have been created. Descartes says that he is a substance, but a finite one. "For although the idea of substance is within me owing to the fact that I am substance, nevertheless I should not have the idea of an infinite substance—since I am finite—if it had not been proceeded from some substance which was veritably infinite."

There are quite a few of us who point out that there have been genocides, mass murders, wars which have devastated whole countries and inflicted unimaginable suffering and terrible pain. As A.C. Grayling puts it in, *What is Good? The search for the Best Way to Live:* The inscrutability of god's purpose, and its propensity to 'move in a 'mysterious way,' are invoked to explain away, such things, but to be asked to accept such non-rational or irrational defences of such apparently non-rational or irrational phenomenon is to be asked to take an even greater risk in placing our trust in the providence. Descartes explains it vey elegantly why we question the existence of God when he says, "—I do not comprehend the infinite, for in God there is an infinitude of things which I cannot comprehend, nor possibly even reach in any way by thought; for it is of the nature of the infinite that my nature, which is finite and limited, should not comprehend it, ——"

With a belief in the Supreme Being, it is easy to accept what ever comes our way, other wise we struggle to find answers to certain questions, especially when a loved one leaves us. Those with a belief in the Supreme Being have no illusions as they believe that both arrival and departure from this world come with the Command and Will of God

Give me death, give me life.

Give me sickness, give me health.

Give me honour, give me shame.

Give me weakness, give me strength.

I will have what ever you give.

St Teresa of Avila (1515-82) Spain

Facing Death

What one has to leave here, one thinks to be permanent

What must happen, (That is death) one thinks to be far away.
(Guru Granth Sahib).

We must remind ourselves that death can come at any time. Guru Nanak says that 'we are people of one breath only' implying that we can be sure of the breath we are taking at the moment only, but not the next one. If you breathe out, and you cannot breathe in again, you are dead. *The only thing we really have is Now, the present moment.* Buddha said:

This existence of ours is as transient as autumn buds.

To watch the birth and death of beings is like looking at the movements of a dance.

A lifetime is like a flash of lightening in the sky

Rushing by, like a torrent down a steep mountain.

Guru Arjan Dev ji the fifth Guru of the Sikhs says:

What ever is visible must pass away.

And: *Who ever attaches himself with the shadow of the tree:*

Repents when the shadow (which is temporary) passes off

Guru Gobind Singh says that he has seen people with wonderful horses capable fleeting at a great speed and bounding like deer. Countless kings having large armies and big power, where others stoop and bow before them. They might have been powerful emperors, but they departed barefoot in the end to the next world. People may be powerful or with no power at all, but the Grim Reaper visits us all.

"The Lord moves in mysterious ways;" is used to explain and justify a lot of experiences in Christianity.

When we open our newspapers in the morning, or switch on the television, we see death every where. It is not something new; wars have been with us for centuries. Yet did the victims of internecine wars, or wars between different nations expect to die? The soldiers with their modern weapons go to war to kill the soldiers on the other side and win the war. They expected glory, medals, gratitude from their country men and women and not death. Do the innocent victims who die needlessly expect to die? They expected the combatants to be shot at, wounded and to die. Did the victims of plane crashes and car accidents expect to die? They took life for granted as we do. We hear stories of people we know and people we do not know who died unexpectedly.

We do not have to be terminally or chronically ill to die. We hear of people who were apparently in good health dying as well. Our bodies suddenly give in, break down like vehicles and the results are unpredictable. We can be quite well one day, fall sick and be dead the next. No body can say for sure that they will wake up tomorrow. It is good to remember Rinpoche's advice: "It is important to reflect calmly, again and again, that death is real and comes without warning".

Some people of course, will disagree with me strongly, as they hope to live up to a ripe old age, possibly hit a century. I might be out on a limb here. 'It is just that when living in a house of sand, we consider that our life is everlasting. I can never forget the death of a student of mine in Kenya, over six feet tall, well built and bursting with youthful energy. He dived into a swimming pool and came out dead. Soldiers in the battle field are alive one moment, defending their country or ideals and dead the next. Only yesterday, a friend of mine narrated the story of his mother's death. She was feeling under the weather, so the doctor was called. As the doctor was prescribing a medicine, she took two deep breaths and was dead.

Patients in a debilitating chronic condition quite often contemplate death, and make the necessary preparations. They finalize their wills etc. and some resolve their differences with their dear ones as they do not want to leave with any bad feelings. It is possible that they view their rows and quarrels as petty when they know that life on this is very short. Though we value life, we are relieved when people who have resolved their arguments and differences move to the next world instead of suffering a lingering death.

It is possible that a healthier and stronger individual can deal with the issue of death better as they will be less frightened of it when it is 'some distance away' rather than when it is 'knocking at the door'. They can reflect calmly again and again till it becomes an integral part of their lives. If we make it a habit to think about death and dying occasionally, it would remind us of our finality, and about the real purpose and meaning of life.

Simple people with not much education, sophistication, social ties and money seem in general to have somewhat less difficulty in accepting their mortality than people of affluence who lose a great deal more in terms of prestige, power, luxuries, comforts and material goods.

In accepting life as it is now, we need to look whether it is a productive life, with a meaning, of service to others. When there is such an acceptance, there is no fear of death. When one is contemplating death, it is difficult to indulge in wrong deeds. Death shows how little time we have. There is a yearning to realize the meaning and purpose of life. This yearning is life itself, to grow and flourish whilst being conscious of self realization. The five evils, lust, anger, avarice, worldly love and false pride are under a degree of control. All foes become friends and one feels enmity to none. (Guru Granth Sahib). When one is not attached to material possessions or worldly love, there is not much concern about death either. Some people like Kabir even welcome death as he says: "Only by dying, can one attain eternal bliss."

It is not simply putting the thought of death in one's mind once in a while; it is going into the heart of what we fear death to be—the end of all that we consider to be precious to us. When you are indifferent to worldly love, material possessions have no hold over you, and then death is not that frightening. Once the fear of death is reduced or gone, we learn to bear grief honestly and courageously. The sorrow that fills the heart when bad news is received will abate as there can be nothing worse than death. You will be able to stand up again what ever the circumstances as human beings are strong. Once we learn not to fear death, we also learn how to live, how to embrace joy and our pain.

We awaken in ourselves the possibility to live our life as it is, with its ups and downs. We learn how to face everything that is thrown at us with equanimity.

Dealing with Grief

When people we love die, it is very hard to bear the loss and it can hit us in unexpected ways. Grief is a deeply personal and traumatic experience. Belief in God or the immortality of the soul can help us cope better with a loss caused by death. Yet we cannot deny or diminish the feeling of loss created by death. We still experience sorrow and we grieve.

How can we deal with our grief? How can we help others who are grieving? Writers like Dr. Elizabeth Kubler-Ross (*On Death and Dying, 1969*) with a psychological leaning have identified several stages of grief, including denial, anger, bargaining, depression and acceptance. But it is worth remembering that a person in mourning may not experience these sequentially. There is no timetable for working one's way through. Some people may feel several of the stages described further up but not others. Some grieved people may experience various stages simultaneously. Someone can go through a stage, and then return to it. People experience grief differently, some recover relatively quickly from the loss, and others take a much longer period to recover fully.

Stages of Grief : Denial

When grieved ones experience denial, their physical responses might include sweating, faintness, nausea or a racing heart, just as with any other victim of shock. The mind and emotions become overwhelmed. Some may not be able to deal with the reality of death. Some may withdraw from the world around them. Others report feeling as though it is a bad dream and that they will soon awaken from it. Perhaps this is Nature's way providing us a protection buffer. It's during this time they can begin to sort out and process our feelings, at their own pace and within the comfort zone.

At such a time those who are grieving often lose sight of their own physical needs. Caring for their personal hygiene, their health, or well being is so often the last thing on their minds.

Stages of Grief : Anger

Once denial loses its hold, our natural tendency is to want to blame some thing external or some body—for our loss and pain. The anger can be with the deceased for deserting us when we really needed him or her. We may be angry because of the timing of the death or even the place of death. When grieving, anger might be directed toward the hospital staff, medical or nursing staff, other family members and even God. Some times we hear people who believed in the existence of God saying that they have lost faith in God. They wonder why God had to take a dear one when death could have struck some body else.

Stages of Grief : Bargaining

Critics say that we do not love God, but are always doing business with the Supreme Being. We go to a church, mosque , a temple or Gurdwara to bargain, please give me what I desire and I shall donate X amount of money or do some good deed like helping a charity.

When we are grieving, some want to make a deal with God as well. They imagine that if they promise to do this or that, God will intervene and put life into the deceased person and things will be as they used to be.

It is at this point that those who are grieving often begin their understanding of their loved one. This is a normal part of the healing process. They gradually realize that there is no bargaining with death, it is only through recognising the situation as it is, of accepting the facts that the reality of death can be turned to hope and normality.

Stages of Grief : Depression

Reality eventually sets in, but we can plague ourselves with the thoughts of what should have been or could have been. If you suffer from depression, one thing you will be aware of is that it is far more than feeling down. In fact, depression affects not only how we feel, but how we think about things, our energy level, our concentration, our sleep, our libido.

According to Paul Gilbert in *Overcoming Depression—A self-help guide using cognitive behavioural techniques,* the central symptom of depression is called 'anehdonia'—derived from the ancient Greek meaning 'without pleasure.' Life seems empty, we are joyless. But—and this is an important but—although we lose the ability to have positive feelings and emctions, we can experience an increase in negative emotions, especially anger. We may be churning inside with anger and resentment that we can't express.

Other very common symptoms are anxiety and fear. When we are depressed, we can feel extremely vulnerable. Things that we may have done easily before seem frightening and it is difficult to know why. So the two 'A's'—anger and anxiety –are very much part of depression.

For many, this could be the most difficult stage to go through. All depressions are not the same. There are a number of different types. One that researchers and professionals commonly refer to is called 'major depression.' According to the American Psychiatric Association, some of the possible symptoms are:

- Low mood
- Marked loss of pleasure
- Significant change in appetite and some loss in body weight.
- Sleep disturbance
- Loss of energy or feeling fatigued every day.
- Low self–esteem, tendency to feel guilty
- Loss of the ability to concentrate.
- Thoughts of death and suicide

Stages of Grief : Acceptance

Gradually, as we deal with our grief, we come to understand and accept that we do not have any other option except to accept the reality. But, rather than let it defeat you, you are looking for ways to move on. We come to a semblance of normality or a new normality. We try to adjust to new realities because the situation has changed. Some people become stronger, deeper and better after facing the great difficulty, and overcoming it. You have resurfaced to face life after the big trial. Emotional balance or some form of equanimity returns very slowly, as wounds take time to heal.

As indicated earlier, the time required for the healing process can be different for each person. Some will feel the loss for a long time, and some will still experience emotions such as guilt, depression or anger. The feelings are to be expected; they are normal.

Solomon's wisdom comes through his observation, "To everything there is a season, a time for every purpose under heaven...a time to die; a time to heal."

Suicide

Man's ability to kill himself has been a source of fascination and fear since the beginning of human history. Sociologists from the beginning of the 19th century to the present day have contributed a great deal to the study of suicidal behaviour. Though often difficult to assess, intention becomes a central issue in categorizing death in which the deceased becomes an active agent.

The World Health Organisation has noted that over one million people commit suicide every year, and that it is one of the leading causes of death among teenagers and adults under 35.

Even though according to statistics, more people die by suicide annually than are murdered or killed in war, it is believed that there is under-reporting of the incidence of suicide because of a desire by families and general practitioners to conceal suicidal deaths in some cases. Various studies suggest that the order of magnitude of under-reporting is more than 50%.

Why People Commit Suicide

Some of the factors which lead people to kill themselves are: depressive illness, shame, unable to achieve expectations, lost love, downturn in career (amongst celebrities), severe money problems (associated with shame, gambling, addictions), some despoiling (disfigurement, paralysis).In such cases the ultimate control over one's life is when to end it.

Of the various hypotheses that have been advanced, the social cohesion theory developed by Emile Durkheim, the French sociologist and his followers still retains the widest support. According to this view, social cohesion minimises the risk of suicide, where as situations in which individuals are dissociated from their groups succumb to egoistic suicides. Durkheim also resurrected the term *anomie* from Greek, (literally without law) to denote a condition of society where there is lack of usual social or ethical standards. More loosely used, it is a concept akin to 'alienation': to describe a condition where an individual has lost his traditional moorings and is prone to disorientation or psychic disorder. The precise meaning of notions such as social cohesion or anomie is debateable, but it is empirically true the suicide rates are particularly high among the divorced, among childless women, among those living alone, the retired or unemployed, and where populations are highly mobile or subject to economic certainty.

Some times the motive is to inflict revenge on others who have wronged them because of self-centredness or maliciousness. They want the 'wrongdoer' to experience guilt and remorse over the death.

A cultural or social factor not unknown in some communities holds that death is to be preferred to dishonour. A man in such communities is considered dishonourable if he cannot protect his property and womenfolk. *Izzat* or *garyat* (honour, respect) is cherished as a masculine quality and is essential to their collective consciousness as individualism is to American or European self-identity. People from the Indian subcontinent have been known to kill others they perceive to be responsible for their *bayizzti* (dishonour, disgrace) or kill themselves to relieve some dishonour. They can't envisage being seen as *bay garayt* (dishonourable, shameless) by their community.

While social factors undoubtedly influence suicide rates, patients with conditions such as severe depression, alcoholism or epilepsy all have increased risk of dying by suicide. The predominant view of modern medicine also is that suicide is a mental health concern with psychological factors such as the difficulty of coping with depression, inescapable suffering or fear, or other mental disorders and fears. Patients with terminal illness sometimes kill themselves to escape their suffering.

In short, it appears that social, psychological, and cultural are major factors (though not all) causes of suicide.

Meaning from Suicide—A Case Study

When young he was known as the 'Golden boy' of the family. 'He had a shining personality, magnetism, and the whole family adored him.' Kehar (not his real name.) got married and had two children. His marriage became rocky at this late stage, and his wife left him to live with another man. Kehar was depressed, and people with a depressive disorder have a higher than average rate of suicide. Prior to killing himself, he called his wife and told her exactly what he was about to do and then proceeded to hang himself.

It is estimated that each suicide leaves an average of six people intimately affected by the death, either as a spouse, parent, brother / sister, or child of the deceased person. For a better word, these people are often referred to as 'survivors.'

His mother was grief- stricken. She had lost a loved one, and there was an obvious void which could not be filled. She felt dazed and numb, and others felt difficult to communicate with her. Kehar's cousin sister 'had lived with Kehar and his mother (her aunt) as a child and was very close to him. They were like real brother and sister.' She felt **guilty** 'first and thought that she could have done much more for him.' Some of the questions running through her mind were: How could have I prevented the tragedy? Could I have done or said something that could have dissuaded him from taking his own life?

Davinder's (not her real name) grief was mixed with anger at Kehar for taking the easy way out. Davinder felt isolated as her aunt found it very difficult to come to terms with the sudden death of her beloved son. She was overwhelmed by guilt, grief and anger at the pointlessness of the whole thing.

After a period of bereavement, Davinder accepted the death, but had feelings of emptiness and loneliness. That is the time she decided to stop self–incrimination and to "evaluate her life." She embarked on a search to rethink her life and its meaning. After much soul searching and deliberation, she turned to her religion and decided that only the Supreme Being can be a source of strength in her period of stress. Davinder feels very connected to God and says that since she has embraced her religion, she experiences the higher power of the transcendent Being. She has 100% faith in '*Maharaj ji*' her name for God who according to her is—true emperor, king of kings (In Panjabi Maharaj ji is also a term of respect or reverence). Now she fully believes in:

Your Will is sweet to me

Nanak craves for the wealth of God's Name

(Guru Granth Sahib)

Her religion has given her love, **meaning** and hope, and she wants to help others who may be experiencing distress because of the circumstances they are in.

Dignity in Old Age

The elderly are not a burden but a gift—without them our lives and our society would be impoverished and diminished. They have a right to our resources and our care.

(Archbishop Vincent Nichols-2009)

Advances in medicine and progress in pharmaceutical industry might have helped us to live longer but society still has to learn to take responsibility for the elderly. In this age, people are probably more afraid of growing old and infirm than death. The younger generation want other people or organisations like the nursing staff, hospitals, caring homes, or the governments to look after the elderly but not themselves. There are very few societies where the elderly are not neglected or abused.

Elderly people have a right to dignity and decent care but are being neglected by society. Quite often the younger generation 'shove' the elderly into a corner, so that they do not intrude in their lives. Dignity of the elderly people will only happen if we celebrate growing old instead of fearing it. There needs to be a fundamental shift in society's attitude to the elderly. It is not difficult if we all remember that we are growing old each and every day. Children of today will grow into young men and women of tomorrow and the younger generation will grow old sooner or later. We all need to set an example. If the younger generation of today treated their elderly people with respect and dignity, there is a big likelihood that the next generation will accept responsibility for them and not 'shove' them into a corner.

When ever I have gone to India, I have heard this interesting anecdote or story with slight variations.

A couple put their elderly father on an old bedstead and shoved him into a corner. When the old man died, the couple's son said to his father, 'Dad, please do not destroy the old charpoy.'[1] When asked the reason for the odd request, the son said, 'I need the charpoy so that I can put you on it when you are old.

We reap what we sow.

Farid, the farmer plants the *kikar* (acacia, Arabica) but wants the grape tree of Bajaur.[2]

(Guru Granth Sahib).

The elderly also have a responsibility. In old age, people's minds show a tendency to slow down and become more tranquil. The philosopher Bernard Russell compared this stage to a rapidly flowing river that rushes headlong through the mountains. But by the time it finally merges with the sea has become slow, broad and placid. At this stage of life, when we are approaching the end of our journey in this world, people should have gained some measure of control over the five evil passions (lust, excessive anger, greed, worldly love and false pride). They might have 'gained some release from a lot of mad masters as the desires lose their intensity.' The delusion that they are here for a long time has been shredded and is replaced by the clear recognition that death is around the corner. So in old age if people do not delude themselves, but instead have character—they are sensible and good tempered, old age will be easy to bear.

Character is a virtue that is indicative of moral strength, personal integrity and conscience. Our words and actions are manifestations of our character. Humility, acceptance and fairness are important components of character. Staying in touch with the power that comes from character diminishes our fear, tension and anxiety about the future. Elderly people have experience; they have climbed more rungs on the ladder of life than the young people, who may look up to them for guidance. Younger people, who need the experience of life, want to know how they can grow and develop, will be prepared to listen to elderly people of good character. The elderly should not preach only, but model what they preach.

But most elderly people harp on the miseries old age brings and some of course seek release from the vicissitudes of the embodied condition. They hanker for the pleasures of their youth, their energy, their achievements, and how they sacrificed for the family. Memories play the usual tricks on them, or because of the weaknesses of old age, they remember the good times, and very little about the wrongs done and regrets they had harboured. They only recall that life was good then, and, nobody shows respect for their old age now. They can hardly be said to live at all and some take the view that they would be better off dead. Such people need to accept reality; the way things are and not live in a fancy world or in the past.

Acceptance enables you to let go what you can't control, like age catching on, and to take charge of what you can. This can be your health, your relationships, your adherence or acting on your values. Acceptance also can mean making do with what you have. Doing exercise on a regular basis or keeping in shape can delay dependency on others.

In old age, we need to remember that we have passed the twenties and thirties when the quest or capacity for self knowledge and reflection is very little. It is the time for making sense of lifc if it not already done. It's also the time to be analytical, for spiritual uplifting or giving life a meaning. The great line from Socrates explains it very elegantly: "The unexamined life isn't worth living."

They talk about death, but do not contemplate death or face the thought of death. In their heart of hearts, they still think that it is far away. What is perishable is still considered as permanent.

What he has to leave, he takes to be everlasting. The death which must happen, he considers to be very far.

(Guru Granth Sahib).

Those who contemplate death, make preparations for departure to the next world, just like we prepare for a journey. If they have wronged anyone, they try to make reparations for it. The man who finds that in the course of his life, he has done a lot of wrong often has a life of foreboding, of pain and suffering. The person may want to resolve all the conflicts, build damaged relationships and clear the unpaid debts. Some become very conscious of donating to good causes or to charities. The spiritual aspect would be paramount in the elderly person's mind, and they may want to get to know the Supreme Being a bit more. They may find comfort in their faith, in some related verses or seek counsel of those that they consider more spiritually enlightened or closer to God than themselves.

Some elderly people may undergo a quantum change which seems to connect or reconnect them directly with something that transcends them and unites them with all of humanity and life. Spirituality may become the lens through which they now perceive all life.

Five Steps to Life Before Death

1. Live in the present. 'Now' is a wonderful gift. Don't waste it on dwelling on the past. Tomorrow may never come.

2. By not talking about death with someone who is dying, we may lose our chance to make the most of the time we have with the person. The person would also appreciate it as they would like to leave everything in order before their departure from this world. It will be difficult but it will mean that when they do die we will have done our best, and really listened to them.

3. **Try to accept that death has happened** when a close relative or friend dies. If we keep on asking, 'Why?' we are putting off the grieving process and incorporating the event into our lives.

4. Use the death of a person as a learning experience, and try to be conscious of your mortality. Contemplate on your own life to make it more meaningful. Live your precious life to the full until such time as you too pass to the other side.

5. Learn to face death instead of fearing it. '*Think not disdainfully of death, but look on it with favour; for even death is one of the things that nature wills.*' (Marcus Aurelius Antoninus)

Footnotes

[1] Charpoy: Light weight Indian bedstead or cot made up of webbing stretched on a four legged frame. Hindustani-*charpai*-four feet.

[2] In North West Frontier Province- Swat valley. The grapes of Bajaur are reputed to be very sweet.

Chapter 2

Religious Beliefs

In the adoration and benedictions of the righteous,

The praises of all the prophets are kneaded together.

All their praises are mingled into one stream,

All their vessels are emptied into one ewer,

Because He that is praised, is in fact, only One.

In this respect all religions are only one religion,

Because all praises are directed toward God's light.

(Jalil al-Din Rumi) Persia

Some may find the above saying very disputable. But religions have stressed compassionate lifestyle that enables us to break out of the prism of self-hood. They have introduced us to a different kind of knowing which 'drives us out of ourselves.' That is not to say that all the faiths are the same. As Karen Armstrong says, 'each tradition formulates the sacred differently and that will affect the way people experience it.'

In the past religion was important to people because they believed that it promoted such things as mental health and inner equilibrium. So in contrast to humankind in former times, we are no longer told by religious tradition what we should do. Over the centuries, adherents of most religions have become distanced from the fire that gave rise to their tradition. The experience is no longer fresh and first hand, no longer theirs, it belongs to their parents or grand parents. It is theirs by heritage only. Some who are looking for an answer to the great question—what is life about? Or, those who seek deeper meaning or purpose turn to religions again. Some have transformed their spirituality within their religious tradition. Others have searched for meaning and purpose outside of mainstream religions because of their belief that differences in religious convictions have fuelled conflicts, bloodshed and war.

I am very aware that many people believe that religion has been responsible for endless wars and much human suffering. Those who attack the religions confuse the issue when they choose to dwell only on the negative aspect and talk about 'harm' only in contrast to the benefits derived by humanity. It's important to note that there is a difference between the religion itself or the essence of the religion and the people who might use it to for their ends. There is a big difference between religion and the religious. It would be wrong to say that where religions are involved in conflicts, religious beliefs are the *only* cause of them. Conflicts are brought into being by a number of factors, politics and ideologies being the main ones.

We will never know if it is divine intervention by scientists, but in September 2009 Professor Bruce Hood psychologist at Bristol University presented his findings at the British Science Association annual meeting that shows that human brain is hard wired by evolution to believe in God. Religion became a survival instinct according to the researchers who studied the way brains develop from childhood and behave during spiritual experiences.

People with a religion thrived compared to their atheist relatives and after many years, the instinct was passed on in their genes. So in other words, what the research is telling us is not only religious belief part of being human but religion has survived so far because it can provide answers to mankind's eternal search for meaning in life—unlike the state, or science.

Practices and customs are an important comfort in life and can often provide optimism and hope for the human spirit. Not knowing what we should do, or must do, humankind feels lost, and sometimes does not know what she basically wishes to do. Not knowing in what to believe and whom to believe, we believe in practically everything. People turn to doctors, professors, and charlatans for answers. The doctor cannot give meanings to a patient, nor can a teacher give meanings to a student. It is possible that we are also looking for the 'truth.' Not being sure of how to resolve the dilemma of life, we do what other people do. There is then existential vacuum. Frankl expresses this dilemma in *Man's Search for Ultimate Meaning* thus: 'Meaning is something "down to earth." However it cannot be denied that there is also some sort of meaning that is "up to heaven, as it were;" some sort of ultimate meaning that is; a meaning of the whole 'universe' or at least a meaning of one's life as a whole ; at any rate a long range meaning.'

It is characteristic of humanity to take something basic and transform it in such a way that it transcends the purely pragmatic. Karen Armstrong explains the transformation and transcendence thus: "Cooking probably began as a useful survival skill, but we have gone on to develop haute cuisine. We acquired the ability to run and jump in order to get away from predators, and now we have ballet and athletics. We cultivated language as a useful means of communication and have created poetry. The religious traditions have done something similar with altruism. As Confucius pointed out, they have found out that when they practised it 'all day and every day', it elevated human life to the realm of holiness and gave practitioners intimations of holiness."

Religious beliefs have influenced the history of the world. They have created seminal strands of thoughts and determined moral codes in different countries. This chapter looks at the core ideas of some principal traditions and significant quotations from Buddhism, Christianity, Hinduism, Islam, Judaism and Sikhism in the firm hope that their central advice will make our lives more meaningful and spiritual.

Buddhism

Born in a princely family around 586 BC, Siddhartha Gautama led a privileged life, without ugliness or suffering. According to a story, his father brought him up in his palace keeping him away from all distressing experiences. But one day he was driven in a chariot and he saw an old decrepit man. On his second day out of the palace, he saw an invalid, on his third trip a dead man. These sights greatly disturbed him because he realized that the same fate awaited him also. On the fourth day he saw a religious ascetic or holy man who seemed to be completely at peace.

'Watch, observe, and be aware of things that leave with force and might. They are agents of growth.' The sights had an impact on him and he sought to understand why we have to face suffering. He emerged from the protracted innocence as he could see that sickness, old age, and death were miseries that he could not control. Gautama decided to seek truth, knowledge and peace like the holy man. He left his wife and son Rahula, and went to the forest to renounce the world and to practise asceticism. This was the beginning of Gautama's nomadic life of reflection, study and austerity.

Hermit yogis taught him expanded and transcendent mental states. Later still ascetics taught him fasting and other body-conquering techniques. He mastered them all, but found himself no closer to the ultimate truth and escape from the common human experience of transience.

The Path to Enlightenment

Gautama set out on the 'Middle Way' (a common name for Buddhism) between the seductions of comfort and austerities of the forest. He sat comfortably under a peepul tree which was subsequently known as the *Bo* or Bodhi tree. Gautama meditated for some days and finally broke through to perfect Enlightenment. He had full insight into the nature of the world, and saw with total clarity what the nature of transience is and how it can be transcended. Henceforth he was known by the honorific title, 'the Buddha' or 'the 'Enlightened One'

It is said that one day a Brahmin priest came across the Buddha sitting in contemplation under a tree and was astonished by his serenity, stillness and self-discipline. The impression of immense strength channelled creatively into an extraordinary peace reminded him of a great tusker elephant. 'Are you a god, sir?' the priest asked. Are you an angel.. or a spirit?' 'No,' the Buddha replied. He explained that he had simply revealed a new potential in human nature. It was possible to live in this world of conflict and pain at peace and in harmony with one's fellow creatures. 'Remember me,' the Buddha told the curious priest, 'as the one who is awake.'

Liberation from Karma

"I have gone in vain through the cycles of many lives, ever striving to find the builder of the house of life and death. How great is the sorrow of life that must die.

But now I have seen thee, house builder, never more shall though build this house. The rafters of sin are broken; the ridge-pole of ignorance is destroyed. The fever of craving is past; for my mortal mind is gone to the joy of the immortal nirvana."

Dharmmpada x l

The aim of Buddhism is to attain nirvana[1], the eternal realm, liberation from karma—freedom from all ties to this world and its cycle of rebirth. The law of karma is the universal Enlightenment and salvation are interlinked—Buddha's knowledge gained after many austere practices was not simply intellectual knowledge but an insight. His central insight concerned the interdependence and impermanence of all things.

Buddha's teaching was focused mainly on showing how to find the end of suffering. The Sanskrit word translated as 'suffering' is *dukkha*, which can also mean stress, or anguish. He identified the cause of suffering as the afflictions of ignorance and *tanha* (desire) mainly in The Four Noble Truths. The Four noble truths are:

1. The fact of suffering or non satisfaction (*dukkha)*: There are many pleasant experiences in life *(sukha*), but none of them continues for ever, nor can life escape change and decay. What gives rise to suffering is the realization that all things are transient *(anitya).* All existence is transient, and the fact of dukkha is the suffering that transience brings with it.

2. The cause of suffering: As we are all impermanent, dependent beings, we are constantly craving or clinging to things and because our craving is unsatisfied we often feel anger or hatred. The cause of *dukkha* is our thirst or craving (*tanha*) for things in this world. But we do not see what our plight is; we are ignorant; perhaps we are wilfully ignorant (*avidya*)

3. The cessation of suffering: The cessation of suffering is possible. It can be achieved by giving up all thirst or craving for things in this world, ceasing attachment to that which cannot endure.

4. The way that leads to the cessation of *dukkha*—Buddha set out a path leading to liberation from these afflictions.

Commenting on these Four Noble Truths, The Dalai Lama says in, *How to Practise the way to a Meaningful Life* that n order to free ourselves from cyclic existence we need to understand its nature. We need to:

- Know the specific types of suffering involved. Once you know the extent of suffering, and know that this life is beset by misery, this deepens your natural wish to be freed from the pain

- Discover the causes of those sufferings. When you recognise suffering for what it is, as Buddha did, then you will endeavour to discover its causes, the sources of suffering.

- See if it is possible to remove those causes. Not until you have determined the sources of suffering, can you understand that there could be a cessation to it.
- Determine what should be practised. Without decisively understanding that the end of suffering is possible, one might consider the practice of the path to be a fruitless exercise.

The study and instructions point a student in the right direction. The path begins with the need to train oneself. This arises from an inner prompting and an observation of how suffering touches everyone—that all things are impermanent, and there is nothing, which will give one true refuge. The Buddha taught that although humans have free will, the law of karma operates in all directions of human life. Karma is the force created by evil deeds or bad feelings which binds people to the cyclic existence. Through reincarnation, humans suffer the consequences, good or bad of their previous lives. Thus like other religions, Buddha offers both a moral code and a transformational goal.

This world is *Samsara*, the world of suffering. One can move away from the repeated round of births, ageing, sickness and death, which is—in Buddhism cyclic existence or *samsara*. It is possible to transcend the effects of karma by resisting desires, until like an unintended fire karma dies down. Buddhism uses all kinds of skilful means to illustrate how karmic consequence works, how actions in this life affect future lives and how our present life is the result of past lives. The Wheel of Life is used as an analogy for the way in which deluded action leads to more delusions in an endless cycle while we remain ignorant of the 'true mind.'

As he was approaching death, the Buddha said:

Of all footprints

That of the elephant is supreme;

Of all mindful meditations

That on death is supreme.

Bardo

O now, when the Bardo of Reality upon me is dawning!

Abandoning all awe, fear, and terror of all phenomena,

May I recognise whatever appears as being my thought-forms,

May I know them to be apparitions in the intermediate state.

(The Tibetan Book of The Dead)

Bardo in Sanskrit means—intermediate state. In Tibetan Buddhism it is the state after death and before birth. The duration of inter-life state is given (largely symbolically) as forty nine days. Although there are slightly varying doctrines among Tibetan schools as to the nature of the experience therein. Before we talk of rebirth, it is worth noting that 'Out of body' experiences are well documented by scientists.

Bardo according to Sogayal Rinpoche in *The Tibetan book of Living and Dying* is used in every day speech among Tibetans for the immediate state between death and rebirth but it has a much wider meaning. It is through the *Bardo* teachings that we understand what we call 'life' and what we call 'death' — truly are. The moment of death is potent with opportunity because it is then, that the fundamental nature of the mind or clear light will manifest.

There is a caveat though as it is not possible unless the person becomes acquainted and really familiar with the nature of mind through spiritual practice. The subject experiencing these *bardos* is not an unchanging soul, but the constantly changing continuum of consciousness which according to spiritual advancement becomes either sharpened or bewildered after disjunction from the body.

The natural *bardo* of the present life spans the entire period between birth and death. Buddhist teachings emphasise that the 'bardo' of this life is the only one and therefore the best time to prepare for death. It can be done by familiarizing oneself with the teachings and 'stabilizing practice.'

Rinpoche says that *bardos* are periods of deep uncertainty similar to our life. As the world around us becomes more turbulent, so our lives become more fragmented. Out of touch and disconnected from ourselves, we are anxious, restless and often paranoid. A tiny crisis pricks the balloon of the strategies we hide behind.

Intermediate State

The Dalai Lama explains in, *How to Practise—The way to a Meaningful Life* that all beings who are to be reborn as humans pass through an intermediate state between this life and the next. In this intermediate state your body takes on a shape that resembles your body in the next life at five or six. He admits that some do not agree with him and believe that it is not necessarily so. When the intermediate life ends, the bridge to the next lifetime has been crossed. This process is carried out by the subtlest of mind.

Soul

The hour has come to part with this body, composed of flesh and blood;

May I know the body to be impermanent and illusory.

(The Tibetan Book of The Dead)

Life does not end, nor is there a beginning. Buddhists says that there are two wrong views about death: that death is a complete cessation of life; and that the self or soul is, in some form immortal. According to the teachings of Buddhism, no permanent soul or self exists.

The main streams of Buddhism believe that the flow of rebirth or *samsara* will continue until they gain release or nirvana. And they may be reborn as humans or as animals. The outcome is determined by what they have said and done their karmas. Buddha insisted that there is no soul or self being reborn. "There is only the constant flow of moments of appearance, with one moment immediately giving rise to the next, and the consequences of karma work themselves out through the sequence of reappearance." It is a privilege and opportunity for humankind that they can understand this and can direct the flow to a good rather than a bad outcome.

Zen Buddhism

Bodhidharma is the key figure who according to tradition, transmitted dharma (teachings of Buddha) to China. In China, Zen Buddhism was called *Chan* or meditation. Today it is practised in Japan, Vietnam and Korea. *Za-zen* is a term that literally means "sitting meditation", and is central to Zen Buddhism. The monk who brought Zen Buddhism to Japan from China was master Dogen (1200—1253). He taught that to sit in zazen is to let go of our involvement with greed, anger and delusion so that Buddha nature can shine of itself.

Like other religions, death is seen as inevitable, and it shows how little time we have. Zen Buddhism believes that to find freedom in this life, one has to come to terms with death and the suffering of dying. Zen Buddhists have to contemplate the end of our existence as we know it and the fears that surround this question.

The emphasis is on—the unmediated life and death of this moment. Rev. Master Daishin Morgan (Abbot of Throssel Hole Buddhist Abbey) in *Sitting Buddha—Zen Meditation for Everyone* says: "To add anything is unnecessary and will only obscure the completeness of it. One must trust oneself utterly to this moment and be content with the life that is now. In accepting life and death in this way, we let go of everything that we think and believe and love and hate—everything. Then in this moment, there is no concern about death. This is not simply putting the thought out of one's mind; it is going into the heart of what we fear death to be –the end of all we hold on to... The sufficiency of this moment cannot be described; it is empty of everything, even of emptiness itself."

Zen Buddhism indicates that in many cases we are the creators of our own suffering. It is possible to be with pain or discomfort. When we are ill, we accept that we have an illness, and do not add suffering to the pain and discomfort. We do not and cannot run away from it. Most people fear the process of dying more than death. Through experience of za-zen, they come to see how it is possible to endure it, and in-fact endure they do.

Sikhism

The word Sikh means 'learner' or 'disciple'; it comes from the Sanskrit word *sisya.* Sikhs are those who believe in one God (Ik Onkar) and are disciples of the Guru. Sikhism is a way of life, or self discipline coupled with a belief in the unity of God, equality of humankind, faith in the Guru's word and love for all.

The founder of Sikhism is Guru Nanak (1469-1539). The word Guru is a common word in Indian and Asian religions for an inspired and well trained teacher. In Sikhism, the word stands for some one who dispels darkness, a teacher of religious knowledge, or conveyor of spiritual insight and liberation (mukti or moksa). So among Sikhs, the term refers primarily to Guru Nanak and his nine successors. All manifested the one divine light, just as one lamp is lit from another. The belief in the essential oneness of the gurus is central to Sikhism On the passing away of Guru Gobind Singh, (tenth Guru) the Guruship was vested in the Guru Granth Sahib, the Holy Scripture.

Sikhism believes that the Creator who is non-spatial and non temporal has create the world of **time and space.** The *Mul Mantra* (basic sacred formula) is the concentrated and essential Sikh teaching. It is one of the first compositions of Guru Nanak and is placed at the head of the Guru Granth Sahib. It precedes the

Morning Prayer called *Japji Sahib.* It contains the essence of Sikh theology and is beyond translation. It is paraphrased by most authors as:

Ik Oankar	There is One Being.
Satnam	Whose name is Truth,
Karta Purkh	Source and Creator.
Nrbhau	Without fear,
Nirvair	Without enmity
Akal Murat	Timeless in form,
Ajuni	Unborn,
Saibhang	Self existent,
Gurprasad	He is known) by the grace of the Guru (Preceptor).

The one being was True in the beginning, and has been True through the ages. He is True in the present and shall be present True in the future.

Some philosophers and writers believe that this world is only a deception, an illusion. While emphasising the transitory nature of the world, the gurus have rejected the idea of illusion. For a Guru, the world is the abode of the Lord. Since the Lord is true, the world is also true. The world is false only in its transitoriness. Guru Nanak says, 'O Lord! Thy regions are real. Thy universes are real. Thy planets are real. Thy creations are real.

Sikhs are adjoined to imbibe the attributes of God. It is a practical discipline and the teachings are to be translated into ethical action. Like any skill, the religion requires perseverance, hard work, and discipline. If God is 'Truth,' then the followers have to be truthful also in their daily conduct and live truthful lives. Guru Nanak has put it thus, 'Greater than Truth is Truthful Life.' We ask

God for forgiveness, for any wrongs done. 'God has no enemy', or is 'inimical to none.' A disciple then, should learn to forgive others for their mistakes and perceived slights. One does not have to be held captive by the past, keep grudges, and regurgitate the insults. Once they have got rid of their selfishness, and self preoccupation, and constantly remind themselves of the attributes of God, they would not look at others 'as strangers or enemies.'

If a Sikh learned to 'realise' the truth that their most authentic Self was part of the Supreme Being, they understood that it was beyond delusion and death. The devotee has to acquire the knack of thinking outside the 'lower case,' they have to meditate on the teachings of the Guru, not to accept them notionally but experience them vividly. Like any other acquired skill, it bypasses the logical processes and becomes part of the inner world.

A practitioner has a loving fear of the Supreme Being and there is nothing else to fear as the 'I' disappears. Kabir in Guru Granth Sahib illuminates this when he says: "Kabir, by repeating Though, Though, I have become Though. 'I' has not remained in myself.

If they apply the teachings assiduously, mortal men and women can show that they can live on a higher, divine or godlike plane and thus wake up to their true selves

Guru Granth Sahib

Any room in which a Guru Granth Sahib is installed is called a Gurdwara (gateway of the Guru). The scriptures are treated with the same reverence as would be accorded to a human Guru in the sense that it is always placed under a canopy on a dais during the day time and ceremoniously laid to rest at night. It is consulted for daily advice (hokum).

Some Teachings from Guru Granth Sahib

You have become old; but you do not realize (even now) that the time of death has arrived. Nanak says, O mad man, why don't you worship God?

- *Wealth, spouse, and riches (property) and everything else which you deem as your own; none of these will accompany you. Believe this to be true, says Nanak.*
- *One who remains unaffected by joy, grief, greed, mammon (Maya) and ego; is the image of God, hear this, says Nanak.*
- *One who des not terrify others and is not afraid of others; should be seen as the Giyani—possessing Divine knowledge, hear O mind (humankind) says Nanak.*
- *One who is immune from praise or slander, and for whom gold and iron are alike, Nanak says, hear O mind (humankind)! Such a person must be recognised as saved.*
- *Why do you entertain false ego? Realize that THE WORLD IS LIKE A DREAM. There is nothing in it, which is yours, says Nanak.*
- *Realize, O friend! That the world structure is all perishable. It is like a wall of sand; Nanak says it's not permanent.*
- *Be worried only regarding that, which is unexpected. The way of the world is that nothing is permanent, says Nanak.*
- *Kabir desires not heaven but absorption in God.*
- *Everything is settled when the soul blends with God;*

Who dwells in earth and heaven;

When the soul leaving earth goes to heaven;

The soul and God shall meet and happiness be obtained.

Cessation of Life—Death Cycle

Life is not useless or meaningless, though it is transitory. According to Sikhism, life is a journey towards union with the Almighty. The process of trying to be one with the Supreme Being cannot be meaningless.

The human body (life) has been given to you

This is your chance to have union with the Almighty.

He whose doubts are dispelled knows the truth-

This Soul has no shape or outline;

By God's order it was created, and by understanding God's order it shall be absorbed in Him.

If anyone understands the secret of the soul,

It shall only obtain divine happiness when absorbed in God.

There is but one Soul (The soul of the world) which occupies all bodies

Kabir worships that Soul.

(Guru Granth Sahib)

Sikhs believe in reincarnation. Death is therefore seen as the next stage in a succession of lives for those who are unable to achieve equipoise in this life (*Sehj awastha*). They might have lived in other life forms but it is only in human life form that they can experience the love of the Supreme Being.

God is the Treasure-house of all qualities (Gun nidhan). All the qualities emanate from Him. He is infinite so His attributes are Unlimited, but the human soul is finite, therefore its attributes are finite also. The finite self is overwhelmed by mammon (Maya) forgets its essence. The attention is on acquiring more worldly goods, more power, status etc, and not realizing virtues or godly nature is covered by Maya and ego. It experiences births and deaths because the god like attributes have not been realized. Death is much more painful for one who is attached to this material existence, and has not made preparations for the inevitable departure. That is why I suppose we fear death in this materialistic world, or we don't look forward to it.

"Know God, by knowing Him, thou shall become as He (is) When the soul and God are blended, no one can distinguish them."

When the fear of God is produced, all; other fears depart:

All other fears are absorbed in that fear,

If man rejects the fear of God, then he has fear of man,

When he no longer fears man, the fears of his heart flee away.

For one who has established a harmonized relationship with the Creator, death is a call to a union. The union is achieved by those who meditate on the Lord's Name, and acquire god like attributes; they are freed from the birth –death cycle. In Punjabi, *kal* means – time, period. It also stands for death, famine, scarcity. *Akal* means Timeless One that is God. The powerful Time does not consume them.

As it is the reality, one should always be prepared to accept it. Death need not be a frightening experience. 'Death which frightens the world is the harbinger of bliss for me.'

Kabir says, while the world fears death, my heart is pleased therewith.

Since it is only by death supreme bliss is obtained.

(Guru Granth Sahib).

According to the teachings of the Gurus, death is the greatest Reality. 'The days of a human being's stay in this world are numbered.' When something is sure to happen, then it should be accepted philosophically:

Be worried regarding that which is unexpected;

This is the way of the world that nothing is permanent, says (Guru) Nanak

(Guru Granth Sahib)

Islam

The Arabic word "Islam" means peace, obedience and submission to Allah. For Muslims, Islam is a way of life symbolized by peace—peace with Allah (God) and peace within oneself, and peace with the creations of Allah and commitment to His Guidance.

Tawhid (oneness and uniqueness of God is to believe in God with all his attributes. God is All-knowing, all wise, and All-Powerful. He created everything that is in the earth, heavens and in between them. He subjected everything to His law after creating it. He is with us all the time. He sees us but we do not see Him. He has no partner, son or daughter, nor has a father or mother; He gives us life and takes it away. Every one must return to Him after death.

Islam is now the second largest religion in the world, and is believed to have over a billion adherents. Its own history began with the revelation of the Qur'an through Prophet Muhammad. Muhammad often used to go from the hustle and bustle of Makah for periods of reflection in a cave outside the city. In 610 he had the first revelation of Qur'an. He heard the voice of the angel *Jibril* (Gabriel) giving him a command:

'Recite the Name of your Lord, who creates,

Creates man from a clot,

Recite, Your Lord is the most Bountiful,

Who taught the use of the pen,

Taught humankind that which they knew not.'

Quran 96:1-5

Muhammad repeated the words until he had learned them by heart. He rushed home and related his experience to his wife Khadijah who said that such lofty words could not have come from Muhammad himself. Khadijah and the Prophet's young cousin Ali were the first people to understand that Allah had chosen 'the trustworthy one' to deliver his guidance. Muhammad continued to receive revelations from God for over twenty years.

Islam like other mainstream religions believes that death is an undeniable natural event for all living things. The Qur'an says that, 'Everyone shall taste death.' Death brings an end to our temporary life on this earth. Human beings cannot predict as to how long they will stay on this earth, only God knows when His servants will die. Death has a purpose, in the sense that a person will behave well and follow Allah's (God's) commands if he remains aware of death and life after death. People mourn for the dead person by reciting the Qur'an and saying prayers. *Isra'eeil* also called Angel of dead (*Malakuul Mawt*) is responsible for ending the life on this earth.

The Qur'an gives a vivid description of the Paradise which will be awarded to the truly obedient servant of God. The punishment to be meted out to the evil doers is also spelt out clearly in the Qur'an.

The teaching in Islam says that God is watching all the actions and people will have to account for them on the Day of Judgement. Man has the free will to choose the course they want to take. As humankind has been given free will, they can choose between right and wrong. This is why a Muslim will have to account for their actions on the Day of Judgement. A person's conduct and behaviour should therefore be responsible and controlled. They should always try to do things which God will approve and refrain from actions which will incur punishment.

Akhira.

"O mankind! We created you from a single soul, male and female, and made you into people and tribes, so that you may come to know one another. Truly, the most honoured of you in Allah's Sight is the greatest of you in piety. Allah is all knowing, All-Aware."

Qur'an 49:13

'*AKHIRA* means life after death. It includes the Day of Judgement and the never ending life after death.' (Ghulam Sarwar). *Akhira* has a tremendous influence on the life of a Muslim. They know that God is watching all their actions and they will have to account for them on the day of the Judgement. Not to care about *Akhira* is a serious failing. As it is certain that all human beings will die, so it is reasonable to prepare for the eternal life which, no doubt will follow death.

The Day of Judgement

According to Islam, the life on this world and all that is in it will come to an end on an appointed day. The Day of Judgement *(Yawmudin)* will follow the resurrection day and every one will appear before Almighty God. The belief in Islam is that there will be a day of reward and punishment. Men and women will be raised from their graves on the day of resurrection. Those who pass the test will be rewarded with everlasting happiness and peace in Paradise (*al Jannah*) and those who fail will suffer terrible punishment in Hell (*al Jahannam*).

Doubts were expressed by those opposed to Muhammad's teachings as to how men and women will be raised after death. The Qur'an says:

"Does man think that we shall not assemble his bones? Yes, surely, yes, we are able to restore the very shape of his finger tips." (75:3-4)

Christianity

The belief common to all Christian denominations is that God entered his creation as Jesus Christ, born as a human being, yet fully divine and that Jesus Christ died to atone for the sins of all people and rose from the dead to eternal life. Christians believe in one God who is infinite. However through the concept of the Trinity, Christians refer to God's three aspects, God the Father (the Creator) God the Son (Jesus Christ) and God the Holy Spirit (the Power of God).

Sin is believed to be the selfish misuse of the freedom given by God, and creates a separation between God and the person who sins. Jesus Christ paid for human sin by his death thereby allowing God and his people to be reunited. The Resurrection is the foundation of Christianity. The first Christians could not in any way explain or even understand what had happened in the Resurrection, but it sent them out into the world to live in the service of others and to spread the good news ('Gospel') that Jesus is alive after death and that he offers to share this new life with others who come into it with faith and trust, and live in the service of others.

What Happens to the Dead?

Christians believe in life after death. Those who place their trust in Jesus Christ are incorporated into his life and gain eternal life. Human beings are judged on their response to God's offer of love in Christ and their conduct towards fellow human beings and God's creation.

Christians believe that God created mankind for a purpose.

Why God Created Humans

God proceeded to create man in his image, "in God's image he created him; male and female he created them." Christians believe that since we are created in God's image, we were given not only physical and mental attributes but also moral and spiritual aspects. and these must be satisfied if we are to be truly happy. God would provide the means for filling those needs as well as the need for food, water and air. As Jesus said, "Man must live, not on bread alone, but on every utterance coming forth through Jehovah's mouth."—Mathew 4; 4.

In the Biblical narrative Adam is the first human being. Some Christians take this as a figurative description of creation. Adam was created in the image of God. In Genesis he is said to have been made from the dust of the earth and to have become a living soul after God had breathed into him. He was given power over the bird, animals, fish of the sea and the plants and vegetables were to serve him for food. Adam was placed in the Garden of Eden, where Eve was created from his rib and became his companion. Eve tempted by the serpent, encouraged Adam to eat the fruit of the Tree of Knowledge of Good and Evil. Influenced by Satan, Adam and Eve made the wrong choice and took of the forbidden fruit, and thus disobeyed God. God could not allow them to live for ever and evicted them from the Garden of Eden.

Human beings are a physical creation. God created Adam from the dust of the earth and informed him, after he had taken the forbidden fruit, "in the sweat of your face you shall eat bread till you return to the ground, for out of it you were taken; for dust (clay) you are, and to dust you shall return (Genesis3:19)

Saint Paul, understands Jesus as the last Adam reserving the penalty of death suffered by the first Adam, and shared, since then by all the Christians. They can reverse the penalty of death by their association with Christ who is believed to be both human and divine. Paul explains how the process in this dimension works.

"And so it is written, the first man Adam became a living being. The last Adam, (Jesus Christ) became a life-giving spirit. However, the spiritual is not first, but the natural, and afterward the spiritual. The first man was of the earth, made of dust the second Man is the Lord from heaven. As was the first man of dust, so also are those who are made of dust, and as the heavenly Man, so also are those who are heavenly" (i.e. composed of heavenly substance) (Corinthians 15:45-48).

A transformation must occur: "And as we have become the image of the man of dust, we shall also bear the image of the heavenly Man."

The Christian faith is based on the Bible which consists of the Old Testament, shared by the Abrahamic faiths; Judaism, Christianity, and Islam, and the New Testament. The New Testament contains the gospels which give an account of the life, death and resurrection of Jesus Christ, and the book of Acts, an account of the early church, and the Epistles written by apostles. The books which belonged to the New Testament were written and agreed in first centuries after Christ. Christians believe that through prayer and the guidance of the Holy Spirit, God's will can be discerned.

Hinduism

Hinduism is one of the oldest living religions of the world. It has no individual founder. The wellspring of Hinduism is the great urban civilization of the Indus Valley. The word Hinduism derives from the Persian word *Hindu*-belonging to the Indus Valley. The area around the river Indus became known in Persian as Hindustan and Muslims after their conquest of northern India, called the non-Muslim population Hindus. Hinduism is a family of related religious beliefs and practices. Some practices and beliefs may not be common to all Hindus as regional differences occur.

In fact the Indian name for Hinduism is *sanatana dharma*—everlasting dharma. The word 'dharma' comes from Sanskrit—*dhr*—which means 'hold' or 'uphold'. It refers to a way of life in which all things and all people ought to behave if the order and balance of the cosmos and of individual and social life is to be maintained. Hinduism is a map of how people should behave properly in what ever circumstances they find themselves.

Hinduism is about 3,000 years old, although elements of the faith are much older. It is not a unified religion, and has no founder, single teacher nor prophets. Hindus recognise a universal soul or God called Brahman as the one supreme all pervading Spirit. Brahman is believed to be the source and originator of all appearances. The Upanishad, one of a collection of Hindu sacred treatise connected with the Vedas, equated the *atman* (Self) with the Brahman (Supreme Spirit) –and developed the theory that as Atman and Brahman are one, the knowledge of Brahman is the supreme goal of a human's life as it confers liberation from ongoing cycle of suffering and rebirth or transmigration of souls.

Any one who is closely associated with a Hindu family would know that Hindus worship many gods. There are many temples dedicated to different deities—gods and goddesses. It is a polytheistic religion. Religions which believe in one God only are monotheistic. With the Upanishads, also came the notion that *Brahman* (the Universal Being) is conceived in two ways, as impersonal, without form, *Nirguna Brahman* or as having physical attributes and qualities, *Saguna Brahman.* As the idea of *Narguna Brahman* can appear so impersonal, and distant, it is easier to make a commitment to one god personifying one aspect of Brahman or *Saguna Brahman.* So each god is seen as a different way of approaching the Absolute. The *trimurti* (trinity), Brahma, Vishnu, and Shiva are three manifested aspects of Brahman.

Hindus also believe that God descends to earth when ever there is an increase of evil; these incarnations are called 'avatars. Vishnu says in Bhagawad Gita: "Whenever dharma is forgotten, whenever lawlessness prevails, I manifest myself in every age. I return to deliver the righteous, to destroy the wicked and to establish dharma." Traditionally there are ten avatars, the most popular being Krishna- the avatar of Vishnu, the hero of many myths.

Three main Hindu gods or Hindu Trinity (Trimurti 'or Three Forms) are:

- *Brahma-* the Creator
- *Vishnu-* the Preserver.
- *Shiva*-the Destroyer

In other words, Brahma creates the universe, Vishnu sustains it, and Shiva destroys it, after which the process starts again. Other popular deities have more specific functions. For example:

- Ganesh, the elephant- headed god brings wisdom and good fortune.
- Lakshmi, the goddess of good fortune and embodiment of beauty.
- Kali, (Sanskrit, - black) many Hindus see Kali as representing the realities of death and time; she stands for the frightening, painful side of life. These are the realties which all those who desire to progress spiritually must face and overcome.
- Hanuman, the monkey-god. He is a symbol of strength and loyalty, and a patron of wrestlers. For a devotee to God, (Bhakti) Hanuman is the symbol of a good servant (dasya) in relation to the master.

Bhagwad Gita

The wise in heart mourn not for those that live, nor those that die. Never was the spirit born; the spirit shall cease to be never. Never was it time it was not...Death hath not touched it at all, dead though the house of it seems! Nay, as

when one lays his worn out robes away, and, taking new ones says, 'These will I wear today!' So the spirit puts its garb of flesh lightly, and moves on to inherit a residence afresh.

(Bhagawad Gita (Chapter 2)

The *Bhagawad Gita* has often been described as a concise guide to Hindu philosophy. For many Hindus, *Bhagawad Gita* is the most revered scripture, the essence of their beliefs. In *Bhagawad Gita* (the Song of the Lord), the question of dharma is central. Bhagawad Gita (The Song of the Lord) is a fundamental text for the Hindus. It is the most revered scripture as it is the essence of their beliefs. Other sacred texts are Upanishads, Mahabharata and Ramayana.

Upanishads contain the philosophy known as the *Vedanta*, concerning the World Soul or *Brahman*. In Hindu belief, the Upanishads are the foundation of true knowledge. The central teaching of the early Upanishads is that the Self (*atman*) is identical to the Brahman who is without attributes, without any characteristics that can be described.

Ramayana is a great epic written at the same period as the Mahabharata and tells the story of Rama's rescue of his wife Sita from the demon king Ravana. Rama is an avatar (manifestation) of Vishnu. Rama and Sita are the model spouses for the Hindus

Mahabharata is another great epic of over 10,000 couplets. The bulk of the text tells the story of the war between two branches of the ruling family. Bhagawad Gita forms part of the book of the Mahabharata and explores the situation which has brought the warrior Arjuna to a crisis of conscience.

The setting of the Bhagawad Gita is a battlefield that symbolises life itself. The Pandawas and the Kauravas are cousins who have assembled on the battlefield to settle the claim to the kingdom of Hastinapura. Realising that his enemies are his own relatives, beloved friends, and revered teachers, he turns to his charioteer and guide Sri Krishna (an avatar of Vishnu) for advice. Offered the assistance of Krishna, Arjuna receives instructions on what he should do, and what his religious duties are.

Sri Krishna counsels Arjuna, beginning with the tenet that the Soul is both eternal and immortal. Sri Krishna's advice to Arjuna is that a man cannot leave the battlefield; he must fight the evil for the good of humanity. The war between the Pandawas and the Kauravas symbolises the war going in the heart of every person. Any 'death' on the battlefield would involve only the shedding of the body but inner soul is permanent. Sri Krishna in the Gita shows Arjuna his dharma (duty) and at the same time shows the path to liberation (moksa). Dharma according to some writers means – Leading a Righteous Life.

According to the Upanishads, the only path to liberation was the Path of Knowledge (Jnana Yoga), the knowledge that the atman (soul) and the Supreme are one. Sri Krishna accepts this path, but says that for people like Arjuna, or for the majority of other people, there is another path. This is the Karma Yoga or Path of Action. Most people perform an action with a desire to gain some personal benefit. Bhagawad Gita calls it the 'fruit'. Sri Krishna says that we are bound to reincarnation because of the desire for 'fruit.' Actions are done to gain the 'fruit.' If the action was done without the thought of fruit, action without detachment, which Sri Krishna calls *nikshakama karma*, and then the actions would have no karmic consequences. Actions are done not for personal benefit but for universal wellbeing. *Nikshakama karma* is a very important moral teaching of the Bhagawad Gita. People should be dutiful (dharma) for universal well being but without attachment to the fruit of action.

Thus Sri Krishna adds the Path of Action (Kama Yoga) to the Path of Knowledge (Jnana Yoga) as a way of obtaining moksa (goal). A person pursuing the Path of Action becomes desire-less, does not necessarily pursue happiness, and as a consequence is not perturbed by adversity. Such a person being unattached, is free from anger and fear. The mind of such a person attains perfect calm.

Sri Krishna also adds a third way to *moksa*, the Path of Devotion (*Bhakti Yoga*) to his teaching of action and knowledge. If a person is a true devotee of God, then God will release him from the cycle of reincarnation.

Marga (path) and Yoga have been used interchangeably. Sri Krishna points Arjuna to three paths (marga), of knowledge, action with detachment, and of devotion to God. Since these are ways of uniting to the ultimately true and real, they are also known as *karma yoga, jnana yoga and bhakti yoga*. Yoga is a Sanskrit word which means 'union'.As practised in the West, yoga is more a system of mental and physical exercise for relaxation and to relieve stress (*hatha* yoga). The Oxford dictionary correctly describes Yoga as a Hindu system of philosophic meditation and asceticism designed to effect reunion with the universal spirit.

An outstanding feature of Bhagawad Gita is its religious tolerance. Sri Krishna says: 'Who ever with true devotion worships any deity, in him I deepen the devotion, and through it he fulfils his desire'. (Chapter 7 Verse 2).

Judaism

Judaism is a monotheistic religion and a forebear of Christianity and Islam. It is based according to the Old Testament on a covenant between God and Abraham about 2000 BC and the renewal of the covenant (solemn agreement) with Moses about 1200 BC. In Jewish belief the Lord was sorry that he had made humankind, and the covenant began the process of God's repair, showing how life might be lived and how it ought to be put right when things have gone wrong. The covenant is the key to understanding the history of the Jews. The basic idea of the covenant is that God offers peace and prosperity provided that people keep to the terms laid down. Both social and individual life depends for their success on living in ways that express justice and mercy. Through the covenant, the Jews believe that they were chosen to fulfil a unique destiny for them to be a holy nation.

Moses was the leader to whom God revealed His teachings including the Ten Commandments. Moses received these laws on Mount Sinai. Here the demand is made that Israel should be as holy as God is holy, and that people should obey the command *Schema*- "Hear O Israel". The appropriate response to God is love, and prayer is the natural expression of love. The *Shema* occupies a central place in Judaism and is a major Jewish prayer affirming belief in one God. It can be said that the basic statement of Jewish belief is summed up in a single verse.

The *Shema:*

Hear O Israel, the Lord (is) our God, the Lord is one. You shall love the Lord your God with all your heart, with all your soul and with all your might. These words which I command you this day, you shall take to heart. You shall teach them diligently to your children. You shall recite them when you are at home and when you are away morning and night. You shall bind them for a sign upon your hand, and they shall be for frontlets (a reminder) between your eyes. You shall inscribe them on the doorposts of your home and on the gates.

(Deuteronomy Chapter 6)

It is recited twice daily in the morning and evening, and the practice dates back to the 2nd century CE.

The religion of the Jews is based upon the Holy Scriptures comprising the Torah and the Talmud. The Torah comprises the first five books of the Bible (the Pentateuch), and contains the history, laws and guide to life for correct behaviour. Talmud is a further source of authority on Jewish ritual, worship and practice. The Talmud contains the original oral Commandments given to

Moses. There are 613 in all, the most famous being the Ten Commandments. The commandments affect all aspects of Jewish life including what they may eat or may not eat. The Ten Commandments are often written above the Ark containing the Torah in the synagogues.

Afterlife

Traditional Judaism firmly believes that death is not the end of human existence. Jews as human beings are encouraged to focus on their tasks in this world. As Judaism is focused on life here and now rather than on the afterlife, it does not have much dogma about afterlife, and leaves a great deal of room for personal opinion. However many Jews prefer the belief in the immortality of the human soul to other beliefs when contemplating eternal life.

The Pittsburgh Platform (statement of principle) declared that: "We reassert the doctrine of Judaism that the soul of man is immortal, grounding the belief in the Divine nature of the human spirit. (It must be emphasised here that this 'statement of principle' was formulated by the Reform Movement and is not shared by followers of Orthodox Judaism.) Rabbi Simmons of Jerusalem says that, "from Judaism's perspective, our soul is as real as our thumb. This is the world of doing, and the "world to come is where we experience the eternal reality of whatever we've become." He then poses a very important and very pertinent question and asks:"Do you think after being responsible for the torture and deaths of millions of people, that Hitler could really **end it all** by swallowing some poison." His answer is an emphatic,"NO". "Ultimate justice is found in another dimension." The next world is called Olam HaEmet—the World of Truth and some writers also translate it as, 'The World to Come.' When a person dies, the judgement is not arbitrary and externally imposed. The soul is shown all the good deeds, and the embarrassing things a person did without any embellishments. It's fully bared for all to see. The person then fully recognises the true purpose of life and the missed opportunities to realize the full potential.

"The rabbis describe the ultimate destiny of the righteous as Gann Eden (Garden of Eden).This is not the same place where Adam and Eve were; it is a place of spiritual perfection. God awards those who keep faith in him not only in this life but in a life beyond death. The opposite of Gan Eden is Gehinnom. There are different views about Gehinnom, but it is generally seen as a place of severe punishment, where fire smoulders unceasingly. Others sources see it as a time when the Jews can see the actions of their lives objectively, see the harm done, opportunities missed, and experience remorse for their actions. The period of time does not exceed 12 months. Only the very wicked are abandoned, and some say their souls are destroyed.

Remeber what has Worked for Centuries

In the film *Krull*, the one eyed giant was from a race born with full knowledge of the time and place of their death. He went headlong into what others saw as danger knowing that it would not be fatal. But he was miserable in this knowledge.

We may not have knowledge of our death, where and when it will happen, but we have new gods. For some people the new gods are football, (in the west) cricket, (Indian subcontinent) and wealth. The modern citadels are the stadiums or football / cricket grounds, the mansions, prestige cars, jewellery etc. We live in an age when we have many possessions but they are not making us happy. The people's search for purpose and meaning goes on.

Some of us have turned our backs on organised religions because of the wars and endless suffering caused by them. It is worth remembering that there is a big difference between religion and the people who might use it to further their own ends. Colin Fry is right when he says that 'there is a big difference between religion and the religious.'

So to come to terms with death, or find meaning and purpose in life, think about the buildings you find in every country and town purposely designed to help people with their spiritual needs. They are the churches, mosques, monasteries, synagogues, temples and gurdwaras that have been bringing comfort and meeting the spiritual needs of the people since times immemorial. If you were brought up in a religion, you might consider going back to it. And even if you weren't, you could read about different religious faiths to find answers to our fears about death, and emptiness in our life. Life may be transitory, but it cannot be meaningless.

Footnotes

Nirvana (Sanskrit, 'extinction'). In Buddhism it is a transcendent state which there is no suffering or desire, and no sense of self. It is the final and attainment in Indian religions, the culmination of the meditative state. Loosely, it is a blissful state.

Chapter 3

The Five Evil Passions

(Obstacles to a life with meaning and purpose)

In Sikh teachings, there are five major vices. They result in suffering and rebirth. They are *kam* (lust), *krodh*, (anger) *lobh* (covetousness) *moh* (attachment to worldly things and *hankar* (ego, pride).

"Five thieves who live within this body are lust, anger, greed, attachment and ego. They rob us of ambrosia, but the egocentrics do not understand it and no one listens to their cries".

(Guru Granth Sahib)

They are quite similar to the Seven Deadly Sins in Christianity which are: pride, covetousness, lust, envy, gluttony, anger and sloth.

Buddhism has three destructive states known as Three Poisons—anger, (which includes hostility and hatred), craving (attachment, clinging), and delusion.

If the emotions and feelings are not managed properly, they acquire such momentum that it is difficult to take our attention away from them and focus on what is really important to us. They take over our lives, and dictate our thinking and behaviour. We forget our search for the real meaning and purpose of our life. As we progress through life, one would expect that we become more relaxed and calm, but instead expend enormous energy to carry enormous grievances, desire for material possessions, and allow our past to affect us every day. According to Sikh view, we find it difficult to build for ourselves a truly worthwhile life because of the five evil passions. People without a religion would also say that these vices rob us of well being, or are a drain.

Now let us discuss these five enemies which hinder our efforts to be true to our fundamental nature and thwart our efforts to lead a more meaningful life. We have a fundamental nature that is pure; children are born innocent, with a clean slate, but acquire some bad habits as they grow up. We get caught up in lust, anger, greed, worldly love and false pride. Once we see these five 'enemies' for what they are, the motivation to be free of them arises. In the cycle of motivation, we may move into the contemplation stage where we want to be have some self-control rather than be slaves of the afflictions.

The Supreme Being has given us the mind and the intelligence to decide what is right and what is wrong—and it must be discerned in each situation. We should also acknowledge that we have all the five evil passions—lust, anger, avarice, worldly love and false pride. It is up to us to cleanse our minds as best as we are able of the afflictions, and act according to the needs of any situation knowing that we are completely responsible for our actions. Each one is ultimately responsible for choosing the right way or the wrong path. Such an approach is empowering as one develops inner resources in the process.

Those who crave certainty, recognition and have power are bound to feel that they need to retain what they have and still need more. Epicurus believed that man's suffering is the result of his passions, his –attraction to vacuous pleasures and his enslavement to the desire for wealth and fame. Some people go into politics for money and power and those have money want to become celebrities and power. People like Robert Mugabe are reluctant to relinquish power because he and his cronies can't imagine a life without power and its trappings. They do not contemplate that they are working for their selfish ends only and not to serve the country or 'the greater good.' Their minds are focused on trappings of power and how not to lose it. They do not cleanse their minds of the evil vices. If they did, they would know that the world has grown weary of greed, exploitation, and division. **They have in their minds distorted the purpose for which we have been created.**

Emotions

Under the heading 'Emotions Keep Us Disgustingly Healthy,' The Daily Telegraph made this report (14 January 2004):

'The emotion of disgust evolved to protect us from infectious diseases, according to scientists. The origin of our emotions has long been a source of speculation and the reason things such as body fluids, cannibalism and incest make us go 'yuck' has long been debated. Today, in the Royal Society journal- *Biology Letters,* scientists provide the best evidence yet that disgust is a protective emotion, as is fear of spiders and snakes that helps to cut our risk of infection. Doctors from the London School of Hygiene and Tropical Medicine conducted a web-based experiment in which 40,000 people reported how disgusting they found a series of pictures including body lesions, faeces, rotting meat and parasites. Disease-relevant objects such as a towel apparently stained with bodily fluids were more disgusting than objects with no obvious disease association...Some people might say that an experiment of this nature was unnecessary, if they had thought deeply about their emotions, they might have come to the same conclusion.

Emotions are complicated collections of chemicals and neural responses, forming a pattern; all emotions have some kind of regulatory role to play, leading in one way or another to the creation of circumstances advantageous to the organism exhibiting the phenomenon; emotions are about the life of an organism, and their role is to assist the organism in maintaining life. Animals have emotions too but they are not widespread outside of the human experience.

'Notwithstanding the reality that learning and culture alter the expression of emotions and give emotions new meanings, emotions are biologically determined processes, depending on innately set brain devices, laid down by a long evolutionary history.'(Damasio, *The Feeling of What Happens: Body, Emotion, and the Making of Consciousness).* What makes one person angry or happy does not necessarily follow in another person.

Emotions don't just happen in the head, the whole body gets involved because emotions have to do with our most important moments –not just what matters with life and death, but with all the profound satisfactions and our revulsions that make us human. Let us take the example of a snake on the footpath, quite a frequent occurrence I must say in tropical countries. It is the body and the brain which interact together. External receptors in your eyes transmit a sensory messages to specific areas of the thalamus, and these then process the signals and send the results to specialized areas of the neo-cortex dealing with the higher stages of the sensory processing, in this case the sight of a snake. The neocortex then sorts out what is going on and alerts the amygdala to initiate an appropriate response. The amygdala is a roughly almond shaped mass of grey matter deep inside each hemisphere of the brain, involved in a range of emotional functions, including the detection of significant events in the environment, fear conditioning and enhancing of storage of emotional memories.

If they confirm that the danger is real, the amygdala is instructed to initiate the appropriate emotional response, not just in the human brain but in the whole body. That is why our immediate reaction is one of fear, you freeze on the spot, and the heart beats a bit faster. It may make some people quiver in their shoes. But then, very cautiously, you take a closer look and see that it is after all, only a piece of rope. Thus, when a rational scan of the situation is also involved, that fear of the snake may not arise, because it is seen to be only a piece of rope, or the snake may be a very small one, resting or retreating very fast. Your brain and the cognitive processes also may calculate the distance, the snake may be real, but is at a distance, not coming in your direction and thus, not an immediate threat.

Emotions don't just happen in the head; the whole body gets involved because emotions have to do with our most important moments, with life and death, and with our satisfactions and our revulsions—that make us human. According to neuroscience, any kind of complex behaviour such as emotion is not based in a single area of the brain. Rather many parts of the brain work together to produce complex behaviour in a person. It is a person who experience emotions, not their brains alone, though brains are the necessary condition for humans to experience anything.

It is the involvement of cognitive systems that is very important. Scientists believe that in general, and far more often, there is cooperation of emotions and reason in a single coordinated response. Reason and emotion together review what is going on, so that human responses are formed from both, as we evaluate the signals from the stimulus. For the benefit of our bodies, there has to be a comparable compromise between automatic responses to emotional stimuli and the rational evaluation of contexts, since otherwise we would be constantly reacting in very irrational ways.

The point is that cognitive processing cannot be separated from emotional experience, because it is involved in determining whether an event or stimulus arising in the external world has some intrinsic emotional effect or not.

Anger

Anger (*Krodha*) and lust are the cause of the gradual destruction of the body.

(Guru Granth Sahib)

Feelings are just as cognitive as any other perceptual image, and just as dependent on cerebral –cortex processing as any other image. To be sure, feelings are about something different. But what makes them different is that they are first and foremost about the body, that they offer us the cognition of our musculoskeletal state as it becomes affected by pre-organized mechanisms and by the cognitive structures we have developed under their influence. 'Feelings let us mind the body, attentively, as during the emotional state, or faintly, as during a background state.' (Damasio)

Anger works against respect for the other person. It is an affliction as it clouds the mind and prevents us from seeing clearly. Quite often we say things in the heat of the moment and then regret them at our leisure.

Anger arises when we feel that we are thwarted in what we want. The latest phenomenon in this age seems to be road rage. It normally comes about because of a conflict between drivers, where one driver feels that the other driver should not be blocking his path. The more powerful a person, the more raged and violent he can turn when somebody tries to prevent him from succeeding in or accomplishing something. "O, Nanak! Haughty and mighty persons are consumed by their pride."

We all encounter trying situations, and quite often lose our calmness when feeling tense and under pressure. When we are angry, we blame others, and rarely dive inside to discern our part in the act. I believe Gandhi once said that when ever he had a heated exchange of words with some one else, on reflection he realized that it was his mistake.

A memory may arise of some one who has hurt me and I find that I am angry. Have you ever watched a dog with a bone? You might have noticed that it will hang on to the bone with grim determination for ages. It refuses to part with the bone or let its owner near it. That is of course natural behaviour for a dog. For a human, hanging on to negative behaviour like a dog with a bone is neither healthy nor a good idea. Letting go of negative feelings is absolutely vital for our well being. You can express your feelings by all means, but by hanging on to those negative feelings about a person or event, you are making yourself feel worse. Do it for long enough and you will find yourself locked into the anger and bitterness. It overwhelms you. You need to learn to forgive, let go of the negative and angry feelings, not to give the other person peace, but in order to find it yourself. Our task is to find the best way of moving ahead with our lives. You have a purpose in life, and it is not to carry a burden of negative feelings. **Forgiveness is the attribute of the strong. The weak cannot forgive**. (Mahatma Gandhi)

We all have negative and positive or fond memories of our experiences. It is wise to retain good memories and maybe recall them once in a while when you are feeling a bit down. Recalling good memories where you did well can be uplifting and boost your morale. Psychologists suggest that if you are not feeling confident in a certain situation; recall a situation where you were fully confident. Your confidence will return, and you can face the new situation in a better frame of mind.

Negative memories on the other hand can be harmful, especially if we indulge in them. The trick is to try to find something positive in an incident which still bothers you. If you can't find anything positive, see if you can learn some lessons so that a similar experience does not recur. Once you have noted the positive aspects of the experience, and lessons have been learnt, try to forget it. To cease from evil is not to feed that anger. This means bringing to an end the rehashing of the incident in its negative state over and over in the mind.

With mindfulness, we can see anger arising and let the anger dissolve in the moment of its arising. Try to live in the moment that is not delving into the past, or what will happen in the future if you don't do this or that. Accept the way things are—when anger arises it is accompanied by thoughts, usually a rehashing of the events that made us angry or a planning / orchestration about what we will do about it. Observe the anger very closely through your own direct observation.

Stress and anxiety can be cognitive or somatic. Somatization is the manifestation of psychological distress by the presentation of bodily symptoms. While we don't think about the stress generated by a situation or a memory, we still experience it. If the physiological symptoms slip under the radar, they can build to a point of burn-out, bringing with it feelings of frustration, despair, emotional exhaustion, and eventually irritability and anger. If anger is not managed properly, it turns into bitterness which can be every consuming.

Buddhists and some psychologists suggest that anger or hatred can be controlled. If anger is taking hold of you, see the anger or hatred as it is, in its naked form, without excusing or blaming any one, either the other party or deflecting it by blaming the circumstances etc. Just contemplate the feeling of anger. Notice what it feels like, observe how it waxes and wanes according to how your thoughts run. It may wane until you think again about the wrong done to you, the harm you have suffered, and off you again. When this kind of thing happens, we are feeding the anger with the energy of our thoughts. Don't stoke the emotion, just watch the feeling.

Set aside the thoughts that are cultivating anger. Do not go on feeding the anger with vicious or malicious thoughts. If you don't feed it, you will find that there is no anger. Be willing to be calm inside, maintain your equanimity through out the process and the anger will soon dissolve; it will lose its grip over you. Although we cannot choose what happens to us in life, we can choose how we respond to what is thrown at us. By becoming aware of our thoughts and perceptions in specific situations and learning to control them, we can develop a direct influence over our emotions.

Some people are proud of their anger, that they can intimidate or frighten other people. Anger over a just cause is fine, where you take some positive action to ensure that justice prevails. In normal circumstances, anger is a defect of a person's belief system, a cognitive problem and an addiction. It is a learnt behaviour that can be eradicated. Excessive anger can thwart you leading a purposeful life as it consumes all your energy and can spoil your equilibrium or *Inner Peace.*

Has anger any purpose in our life? What nature gives us is not necessarily the impulse to attack the other person, but to deal with the obstacle or the 'problem.' We can observe that when angry, we do not deal with the obstacle but instead deal with it in a hurtful fashion with the person who is causing the obstacle or 'problem.' It's a learned element of anger that becomes automatic, and we have to unlearn it.

'Compassionate anger' might be a rough state of mind, but it is not hatred. Though it expresses itself as a type of anger, the main motivation could be to seek justice or put an end to injustice.

Hatred

'An eye for an eye makes the whole world blind.'

(Mahatma Gandhi)

Hatred is closely associated with 'anger.' Nelson Mandela spoke about racial hatred in Cape Town in 1990 thus: 'No one is born hating another person because of the colour of the skin. People must learn to hate, and if they can learn to hate, they can learn to love, for love comes more naturally to the human heart.'

Hatred ceases when it is replaced by love. This is an unalterable law as you cannot despise or hate some body that you like or love.

Conflicts

If you are patient in one moment of anger, you will escape a hundred days of sorrow.

Thomas Hobbes (1588-1679) identifies one very fundamental principle: human beings have a powerful drive to increase their happiness by satisfying their own desires. Unfortunately, in their natural state, the drive brings individuals into conflict with each other. We often desire the same thing, and because the desired things are in short supply, competition and conflicts ensue. As each human has the power to kill any other or take what they want, or protect what they have, then violence, or at least the threat of violence, is never far away. And so, in the state of nature, each person lives in perpetual fear of a provoked or even, unprovoked attack. As a result, the life of man is, as Hobbes put it, 'solitary, poor, nasty, brutish and short'.

Disagreements do happen, but they are best resolved at the earliest opportunity before they grow and fester. Quite often we say that time is a great healer, and after sometime, the dispute will lose its intensity, decline in significance and everything will be back to normal. In most cases, what seems important today may not seem that important six months later. This certainly applies to people who live in the present, or want to move on, and do not dwell on the past. But most of us do not subscribe to this philosophy, and there are people who will hold on to an insult or a perceived insult for a long time.

A house which is not cleaned looks dirty, and if the clutter is allowed to accumulate, it takes over the house. Similarly people, who have dwelt upon the perceived insult, are full of venom, malice and hatred. A casual observer can feel their tenseness, their readiness to fight and if necessary provoke the other party. There is no understanding of the other person's view point or position, no compassion for themselves or the others, their minds are centred on revenge. 'The blame lies with the other person', and hence, there is resistance to personal introspection because of the conviction that it is the other party who is in the wrong. As they are consumed by hatred, they cannot see the wider picture. Their prime aim is to harm the perceived enemy, physically, materially and psychologically.

If one thinks deeply, such people are not really in charge of their life. Their attention is on the other party, waiting for them to make a wrong move, utter a word which can be seen as disrespectful so that they can jump at them. When one constantly talks about the other party, lists the catalogue of wrongs done by them, then she loses her identity and her soul too. There is no other purpose or meaning to life except revenge. You can often hear such afflicted individuals say that 'revenge is sweet' when they achieve it.

Such persons are not in control of their life, the other person is, because the other party can wind them up any time they want. They focus on the other party, instead of looking inwards and analysing their own contribution to the ongoing saga, they are brooding on blame only. Instead of developing a compassionate nature, they become vile and isolated. Such persons are defined as the enemy of, 'so and so'. Anyone who communicates or is friendly with the 'enemy' is with the other party, and can never be their friend. They find it difficult to appreciate that some people want to be friendly with both the parties and to be neutral. They fear to let go of the animosity because that is their *raison d'être*, (reason for being).

Agony aunt columns often have questions as to what friends of a couple who have separated under acrimonious circumstances and treat each other with great suspicion should do. If they visit Joe then, they arouse Mary's ire and if they happen to visit Mary, then Joe doesn't want to know them. Some friends face a dilemma in such situations.

What Happens?

Rather than a dialogue, the dispute becomes a confrontation with neither side listening to what the other is saying. Small misunderstandings become dreadful misunderstandings, and an ordinary discussion becomes a heated argument. There is no hint of the spaciousness that such a dialogue requires, let alone the friendliness essential to reach common ground.

To understand the other person, we need what Confucius called an 'attuned ear.' An attuned ear is 'the ability to listen to any words, no matter what kind of words they are, and when looking at an issue, to always take the point of view of the other person who spoke the words.' An 'attuned ear' has to make itself infinitely open and expansive, be able to make minds at different heights, and not stubbornly stick to one's view point or remain at the same height.

There is an old saying: Two clouds can only come together to produce rain when they meet at the same height

TOP TIPS TO AVOID CONFLICTS

- Value yourself and others.
- Care about how other people feel. Learn to empathize. Empathy—is the, 'the ability to understand and share the feelings of another.'
- Recognise how emotions can affect behaviour; and be aware of how your behaviour can affect you and others.
- Develop your Emotional intelligence.
- Value co-operation, negotiation and mediation.
- Practise listening, communication and co-operation skills.
- Realise how agreeing on 'Ways- to –Behave can help build better relationships.
- Go for win-win outcomes.

- Take account of different points of view from your own.
- Develop skills in building positive relationships.
- Find and choose different ways of reacting to angry outbursts / aggressive behaviour.
- Learn how and where to get help and support.

Making Amends

If you have hurt some one, taking responsibility for our mistakes is redeeming. You don't have to whip yourself, as guilt does not encourage us to change in positive ways, but debilitates us. Making amends is more than just saying sorry, though some people find it very difficult to say 'sorry ' also. According to Colin Fry, in *Life Before Death*, "It involves a willingness to listen to another person's hurt and take corrective action where possible. We and our relationships must be transformed as we change our future behaviour patterns..... We still have to live with the consequences of anything we do; at the same time no-one is beyond redeeming their past actions, and making amends in the correct manner will add meaning and purpose to the remainder of our lives."

We all know that our physical bodies do not last indefinitely. Our journey on this earth is temporary. There is no need to continue to hate and bear resentment or punish your self with guilt. Stop sweating the small stuff. Resolve any arguments or differences that you have with family members or dear ones **now** and live your life as meaningfully as possible.

Choice

People who are involved in a conflict state that they have no choice, the other party is provoking them, and the protagonist initiated the whole thing and so on. According to Jean-Paul Sartre, (1905-80) human beings are free. 'Man is condemned to be free'. 'This freedom can be an enormous burden and responsibility, so we deceive ourselves, pretending that, like mere physical objects, we are wholly predetermined to be what we are and behave the way we do'. Sartre thinks that the fact that we have the freedom at each moment to break free from all our old habits and choices and forge ourselves anew is something we are well aware of, at some level.

What purpose we have in life, and how we act, must be freely chosen by us. The responsibility to choose is unavoidable. A person is not determined to be or do anything in particular in the way a mountain, tree or up to a certain extent an animal is. We are at every moment, able to break free from our old habits, and the roles society has handed us. You are able right now, to choose different values, find new goals, react differently, forge yourself anew. Nature has given freedom to humankind, as we are rational beings. We have the freedom to choose, to change, and to be other than what defines us.

The fact that we have the freedom at each moment to break free from all our old habits and make rational choices and forge ourselves anew is something we are well aware of at some level. Sartre thus confronts us with the unavoidable responsibility to choose, and expose the deceptions we perpetrate on ourselves in order to try to avoid it. A level headed person, who has a sense of responsibility, will choose a response which is correct under the circumstances, because it will come from a moral high state. Sartre may sound too definite, doesn't leave us with much choice, but irresponsibility will not lead us anywhere also.

The following tale in Buddhism illustrates that when it is time to put things down or let old thoughts and grievances go, put them down and let them go.

Two monks came down from their mountain temple to beg alms. When they reached a bank of a river, they saw a girl, who was upset because she was unable to cross it. The old monk said to the girl: 'I will carry you over on my back.' And he gave the girl a piggy-back across the river. The young monk was shocked to do any thing more than gape in astonishment. He didn't dare to ask any questions.

They walked on for another twenty leagues, and at last the young monk could bear it no longer, so he asked the old monk: 'Master, we're monks, we are supposed to be celibate, how could you carry a girl across the river on your back? The old monk replied calmly: 'You saw how I got the girl across the river and put her down. How come you have carried this thought with you for twenty leagues and yet you haven't put it down or let it go?

If I try to take revenge, I will torture myself. I have to focus on my life. The past is the past, we can't live there. (A prisoner of Guantanamo).

Develop A Positive Attitude

Misfortune comes from one's mouth and ruins him, but fortune comes from one's mind and makes him worthy of respect.

(Major Writings of Nichiren, Vol.1)

- A positive attitude will help you to cope more easily with the ups and downs of life.
- Don't think of conflicts and negative occurrences as abnormal. Treat them as a normal part of life and then they will be more manageable.
- *You are what you think.* Positive thinking means welcoming into our mind thoughts, words and images that are helpful to growth, success and accomplishment. We choose whether our reactions to an event are positive or negative, enthusiastic or dull, beneficial or harmful. You cannot choose what happens to you, but you can choose how to react to it.
- If you find yourself struggling to replace your negative thoughts with positive ones, do not give up. There is no barrier to the possession of noble thoughts, and as long as you are striving for these, your life will have more meaning.

- No matter what you feel someone has done to you, you must learn to let go. Don't let your life be destroyed by bitterness and anger. When you let go, only then you are living in the present and not in the past.
- Forgiving someone does not mean absolving them of their responsibility. It means letting go of the past; the pain and hurt you feel in your heart and reclaiming control over your life. It's not a favour to the person who has wronged you; it's a gift to yourself.
- Think about what you can do to make others feel more positive. You will be enthused and look at life differently when you realise that you can inspire and motivate people. By projecting positivity you will encourage it to come to you. People will sense that you are worth being around, and you will be associating with happy, positive people.

Conflict Resolution

Experts have different theories about the causes of conflicts and breakdown of relationships, but they all seem to agree that human beings are inherently good. So why do we fight with each other? Why do we allow our friends to become our foes? Why do we allow our aggressive and destructive urges to dominate us?

As mentioned above, we are always convinced that the other person is to blame for all the troubles. Lame is the atom bomb of friendships and relationships, destroying everything that gets in its way. People who complain and blame others for their problems in their friendships and relationships never seem to get better. They just keep arguing and fighting with other people, no matter how much you try to change them.

It's not so much that we want to fight, and hurt each other; it's just that we don't know a better way. We all want love and respect, but sometimes we don't want to give them to others especially the ones we are at odds with.

Individuals, who focus on changing themselves, becoming more compassionate, can work wonders. They let go of their own anger, bitterness, fear and their unexpressed emotions. They realise that life is fragile, and want to move on. Once they have increased their empathic skills, learnt the value of warm relationships, they try to clear the differences with the person they were at odds with.

Respect and Kindness : To Resolve Conflicts

- Walk in the other person's shoes. Think how the person you are at odds with would be feeling. This is the first step in understanding the effects of the breakdown on both of you.
- We all want love and respect, but don't want to give them to others, especially the ones we are at odds with. It could be because we are feeling hurt and angry.
- If you look down upon people and treat them badly, they will retaliate and appear to be annoying and hostile.
- Treat them with kindness, and they nearly always will be more responsive to your feelings.
- Let them know that you like and respect them as persons, even though you're both feeling angry or have a disagreement with each other right now.
- Convey warmth and caring through your body language, showing that you are interested in resolving the dispute. Your voice should not be saying one thing and your body another. If you are telling someone that you value their friendship, frowning, crossing your arms, and shaking your head are sure give away signs that your non verbal communication does not match with your verbal communication.
- If you treat people as you would like to be treated (Please see the Golden Rule), make sure that your comments don't hurt or humiliate them, you can get away with saying just about anything.

- If you have to criticise someone, convey respect at the same time, they are less likely to get defensive and ignore you.

Egotism

Those who shed their ego live in peace, but haughty and mighty are consumed by their pride.

Knowledge is not so covetable a property for a true man as a flame in his heart which might consume the dross of self.

(Guru Granth Sahib)

According to David Cook, 'egoism is the moral theory that self-interest or selfishness is the base of our moral views and attitude. When we make moral judgements, we do so on the basis of pleasing ourselves only. The general notion soon takes a very specific form called hedonism.'

The central message of the Gita is 'Nish Kama Karma—that is acting without attachment to the fruits of action. Such actions express love and self surrender. It leads to egoless-ness. Ego-self must be reduced in order to advance spiritually.' The aim is to decrease selfishness or egoism.

Practically all the religions and philosophers agree that 'ego' is one of the great evils, and if it is controlled then other afflictions like anger, greed, lust, pride and attachment can also be overcome. 'The whole objective of the human being is to free the personality from the contraction of Self in desire into Soul in love.' (Tagore) Gandhi believed in 'being egoless' as the highest personal virtue. Some people have likened people who carry a heavy load of pride—full of egotism to donkeys. Donkeys were used as a mode of transport, and in some developing countries still carry heavy loads from place to place. Donkeys have no choice, humans have. Humans can throw off their unwanted baggage any time they want. The baggage would slide off our backs when we try to transform from ego-gratification to altruism and compassion for others.

The Oxford dictionary describes egotism as the quality of being excessively conceited or absorbed in oneself. It is the frequent use of 'I' or self aggrandizement. A.C. Grayling describes 'Egotism' as the 'excessive self-reference of the individual who cannot resist speaking and thinking about himself before all others—who can be said, in short, to suffer from 'I-strain' in both conversation and the transactions of daily life.(*Ideas that Matter—A personal Guide for the 21st Century).*

If you are unwilling to let go of the ego, and its attachments, then it is difficult to understand your true nature. This 'I' is very insecure and wants lot of assurance. It covets wealth, and wants praise, love, assuring. The 'I' or 'self' is aware of its vulnerability and is repelled by what ever it sees as a threat. Anger arises when the ego is threatened or thwarted. We lose our cool when somebody or something is viewed as an impediment to what the 'I' craves. This anger ranges from the mildest irritation to a rage in which we wish to completely destroy others. All manners of delusive states like jealousy and pride have their origin in the 'I. The humble who have subdued their ego live in peace. **He, who is humble and effaces his self, lives a happy life.**

Fear and desire are the main driving forces behind the phantom 'I,' so as Guru Nanak says, "Recognise your true nature." Paul Roland thinks that, 'True luxury is being able to find the time to sit and think about who we really are, where we have come from and where we are heading.'

Once you recognise your 'true nature,' you become aware that you are part of the universe and a ray of the Light, that each human soul is a spark of the Divine. He, who believes in God, sees the vision of God in all things (Guru Granth Sahib). You also become aware that we are on this earth for a purpose. You are more self aware and confident. Most of all, there is a deep abiding concern for others and the basis of life becomes what is good to do, rather than what 'I' want. You want to acquire some of God's attributes who has no enemies, is fearless and eternal.

When one will not remain in this world (for ever), then why consume oneself in ego?

(Guru Granth Sahib)

The spirit is our true holy nature, an aspect of the divine whole, the real us, what some people may call a soul. On the other hand, ego is the absence of true knowledge of who we really are—it is our self- created concept of who we really are based on our responses to the conditioning we have experienced. It cares for appearances and images above all else, and is always focused on the past or future, never now. Nick William says that, 'the ego will have us for ever seeking outside of us what is already inside us. It is rarely satisfied and never at peace, and is at the root of who most of us think we are. Much of our energy is devoted to proving our self-concepts, attacking and defending against anyone who threatens our sense of self.'

We can either be a hostage to our ego, or a host to our spirit. With mindfulness, we can take care of the needs of our ego and be focused on our spirit. When in doubt about a response to a situation, ask yourself if it is ego or your spirit speaking.

Ego says: Be afraid.

Spirit says: There is nothing to fear. True joy and fulfilment come from facing and stepping through fears and no longer letting them control you.

Ego says: I want separation from everything.

Spirit says: Connection with all. Knowing that we are inherently connected makes our life more meaningful.

Ego says: There is emptiness in life.

Spirit says: There is fullness in life. Search for purpose, meaning and connection in life.

Ego says: Withhold. There is lack and scarcity.

Spirit says: There is an abundance of all we need.

Ego says: Other people don't deserve my best and they won't appreciate it anyway.

Spirit says: Transform life by kindness and generosity. Be willing to give and contribute regardless of the reception you get.

Ego says: Look for easy money (lottery). Go for a mine and take all the gold!

Spirit says: Work for everything. Earn your living by honest means.

Ego says: Protect yourself. Attack and defend your position at all costs.

Spirit says: Choose a new attitude, a new response to the circumstances.

Pride

Kabir, be not proud on seeing thy lofty dwellings;

Today or tomorrow though shall lie *beneath* the earth, and the grass shall grow over thee.

Kabir, be not proud, let none laugh at the poor;

Now thy bark is on the sea, who knows what shall happen. (You may become poor or low your self, and people will laugh at you).

Kabir, be not proud on seeing the beautiful body;

Though shall leave it today or tomorrow as a serpent its slough.

(Guru Granth Sahib)

Pride rides on power, knowledge, wealth, beauty, masculinity etc.

The proud ones can normally be noticed; they may be powerful or 'big' and are consumed by their pride. There are people who are proud of their riches and properties. One can have pride of kingship or being very high in a government, and political leaders are normally susceptible to this. One can perform some religious deeds and this can also engender pride as the person sees himself as virtuous.

I am not implying even for a second that one should not perform religious deeds. But the deeds should bear the right fruit, in the sense that the heart or their souls should be softened. Having riches does not necessarily always lead to pride. There are plenty of examples of wealthy people with 'soft hearts or souls' trying to help their less fortunate neighbours. Bill Gates set up a trust using almost his entire fortune with a view to helping others.

Lust

Delight of lust is gross and brief

And weariness treads on desires

(A. Baehrens translated by Helen Waddle)

In English, the ancient root is, *las,* meaning eagerness, from which we also get "lascivious "and "listless." Lust in the past was used for any strong passion, even the desire to be closer to God. Lust did not attract its specifically sexual sense until the 16th century, and the older sense of pleasure and enthusiasm persists in the adverb 'lusty.' In most of the world religions it is an evil passion, an affliction or a sin. In Sikhism it is one of the five passions or enemies and in Roman Catholicism the word for lust was *luxuria*, one of the Seven Deadly Sins.

One can have lust for power, success, celebrity status, wealth and sex.

Greed

Our anxious and acquisitive ways are a symptom of our reluctance to ponder the awful fact of mortality,

(Dr. Williams, the Archbishop of Canterbury)

Greed like a mad dog, bites and infects every one

When there is greed, there can be no love.

(Guru Granth Sahib)

The mind is full of innumerable desires vying for attention. And we become victims of our desires. Desire clouds the mind and distorts reasoning. Contentment is the key to happiness, but we find this unpalatable because we equate that with denying ourselves objects of desire. With a disturbed mind our thinking becomes flawed and actions faulty. Contentment is difficult to achieve, without loosening our attachment to material things. One has to embark on a programme of desire-management.

Professor Loran Nordgren from Kellogg School of Management in Illinois led a study on the 'Power of Temptation,' found that many people overestimated the amount of temptation they could resist. Pride comes before a fall when it comes to temptation. People are not good at anticipating the power of their urges. "This leads them to make poor decisions and participate in impulsive or addictive behaviour." According to Professor Nordgren, "we expose ourselves to more temptations than is wise. So the key is to avoid any situations where vices and other weaknesses thrive and most importantly, for individuals to keep a more humble view of their own willpower."

Ambition is our primary drive. An ideal model would be: When a desire is satisfied, it should lead to Contentment i.e. Desired—Satisfied—Contentment. But the reality is that if one desire is satisfied, it spawns another ten desires. As long as a person is engrossed in desire, they are at the mercy of objects of desire. Christ said, "It is difficult for a rich man to enter the gates of heaven as it is for a camel to enter the eye of a needle." Exegetes have offered different explanations of this saying, but I think it's because a rich man's attention is mostly on his wealth and not on higher values or spirituality.

During boom times in the economy we admire the bonuses paid to investment bankers. No body ever mentions that they are excessive, or should be reined in. Businesses talk about profits they have made, and we look up to people who have made to the top in pressured and competitive environments. A profit making motive is never frowned upon, but appreciated. During difficult times, or when there is a down turn in the economy, some of us stop and reflect. There is perhaps an element of stock taking, and huge profits or bonuses may look obscene. There is nothing wrong in making a reasonable profit, as we all need to feed our families and have a roof over our head. People are in business to make money, but then, it depends as to what use you put it to.

When stock taking, we come to see that greed should not be worshipped, that it is something to be ashamed of also. No doubt as Hobbes said, 'human beings have a powerful drive to increase their happiness by satisfying their desires' but it should not be at the expense of others. A profit making motive—that is making money out of human beings should not be the sole purpose of our existence. When doing a reality check, it might be worth remembering what really matters to us, our values and our mission in life. It could be to ensure your family's happiness, or honesty, or compassion—for self and others.

I do not want to trivialize death, its pain and crushing psychological damage caused to near and dear ones, but it does force people to examine their lives and work out what matters. The realization that materialism isn't enough to satisfy the human spirit might be a good thing. It might ease the pressure on us to get more money and become richer. We can get out of consumerism and embrace spirituality. We do not have to romanticize poverty, but we need to look at greed when it arises.

Worldly Love

One is established in Wisdom when one is everywhere, unattached, neither elated at obtaining good nor vexed with evil.

(Bhagawad Gita)

A truly wise man will not be carried away by any of the eight winds: prosperity, decline, disgrace, honour, praise, censure, suffering and pleasure. He is neither elated by prosperity nor grieved by decline.

('The Eight Winds' by Nichiven—13th Century Buddhist Songs)

For some people, this world is one big amusement arcade, and it is so attractive, so tempting, so inviting, that they are stuck in it, engrossed in it. Such people chase material things from the world and are attached to worldly pleasures.

Some people say that wealth increases the distance between people. The wife of a chief executive says that 'if I want to see my husband during the day, I have to ring the secretary. If we go out to dinner, his Blackberry always comes with us.'

Underneath the skin, we are all similar; we must 'have' what ever the cost. We are hard wired to 'get the goods, what ever they may be: water, bread, (or rice), money, properties, motor vehicles, private jets and … (That is our hierarchy of needs in the right order) When ever we obtain or conquer something, we get a quick hit of dopamine in our system, that tells us, chemically, 'well done' and makes us feel all warm and satisfied about ourselves. Dopamine is a chemical found in brain tissue that acts as a neurotransmitter. The problem is that the effect of dopamine lasts a very short period. Eventually the hit disperses and, if we don't get another hit quickly, we feel bereft. Buying things works on us in the same way that cocaine or crack does, once the buzz is over—you need more. This means we're metaphorically not only always chasing our tails, but always chasing a bigger and better tail. The question we need to ask is: Can I overcome the desire to obtain, conquer or have things?

Attachment

Earning a thousand, man runs in pursuit of millions;

He is never satisfied in his pursuit of wealth.

He indulges in countless evil passions;

But always unsatisfied, kills oneself by hankering after them.

Without contentment, no one is satisfied…

(Guru Granth Sahib)

Normally we say that stingy people are attached to their wealth. They do not enjoy it, but spend all their energy on accumulating it. There are quite a few reports and anecdotes of such people leaving hundreds and thousands of pounds or dollars behind after their departure from this world. No body takes a penny or a cent to the other world.

Attachment has nothing to do with experiencing worldly things. It is the mental dependency on them. Jaya Row in *Profile of the Perfect Person* offers a good solution when she says, "To remain detached, you do not have to sever relationships or physically remove yourself from a person or object. All you need to is retain your inner independence. When your happiness is not dependent on any object or being, you are not attached to it then." For ordinary mortal like us, it is very difficult to attain complete detachment to all phenomena in our life. It is better to aim for balance and to reduce desires or attachment to the least possible level. We can try to get things into perspective so that we are not enslaved by desires or attachment.

Ask yourself, 'Are you attached to your nationality, language, race, personal history, habits, car, and money etc.? You can attract the type of people you want in your life by becoming that type of person. If you want loving people in your life, you will have to be a loving person first. To acquire this attribute, one needs to be self aware and changing parts of the personality that do not love. If one wants to live in a world that is less violent, then the individual must become aware of parts of their personality that are violent and do not nurture them. The process of change is not easy, but it is the heart of spiritual development. We must recognise all that we are, and must not deny any part of our personality.

Some people do not change. They remain angry, vengeful, narrow minded, bigoted through out their lives. They react repeatedly in the same way, because of their psychological and emotional characteristics, and attachment to the same old habits. They create the same experiences and the same consequences again and again, time after time. Other people replace their anger with calmness, with appreciation or lighten up.

When you change yourself and pursue your new values and perceptions, you will no longer be attracted to old friends with the same old habits. When you replace your old habits and characteristics, you will hold the new ones in great esteem, and they will become embedded as well. The attachment to the old ones will gradually dissipate. The process may take time, but you can be what you want to be. Choice is the **power** to make a difference in your life.

We all know that our life is transitory, that we came with nothing and will leave this world with empty hands. Still we place profound value on the acquisition of wealth; I am not saying that we should turn our backs on material possessions. We need money for our subsistence, and we do not have to renounce and live ascetic lives. If we all renounced material things, then we would be mendicants and live on alms only. We have got to be realistic, if we all did that, the world would be a terrible place to live in. There would be no economic, technological or scientific progress in this world and a time might come when there would be no body to give us any alms (charitable donations of money or food) when we go begging. We need balance in our lives. Money is needed for subsistence, but our lives need not revolve around it. It is the hankering, craving, lusting after sense objects that makes us their slaves.

'Whenever a king accumulates, he attaches himself to it, while a seeker is in the process of freeing himself from attachment. One is busy with an outer journey, while the other one is bent on an inner journey. One tries to own the world, the other to own himself. But trying to own the world is a way of destroying yourself. Be the owner of inner light and become free!' (*The Secret Power of Light*)

Non-Attachment

What came to this world with you?

Then why have you attached yourself to worldly pleasures like a greedy moth

(Guru Granth Sahib)

Normally we all say that it's good to achieve, and it's quite natural to achieve success, wealth and fame. We can do an activity without getting into the web of desire. Consider it as a service, and maintain your freedom. If you take it as a service, you are not imprisoned by the very activity you are engaged in. It's not a question of 'what's in it for me?' But the emphasis then becomes, 'How can I contribute?' Your actions are then driven by unselfish desires for the 'greater common good.' The greater common good can be your family, community or your country. In his historic inaugural speech as President of the United States on January 20, 1961, President Kennedy lit a torch for a new generation. The stirring phrases were designed to appeal to America's pride in their country, and raise their awareness as to what they can do 'for their country.' "And so, my fellow Americans, ask not what your country can do for you; ask what you can do for the country."

Psychologists have identified four fundamental needs: to feel secure, competent, part of a community, and authentic. On this basis, one can understand people buying things they actually use – futuristic wooden furniture from IKEA, but not why we are blinded by the glare of snazzy gadgets.

Many celebrities seem to have it all but end up in rehabilitation centres. Their inner world is missing.

May be you need to look at yourself to determine whether you are addicted to have more and more? The following questions hopefully will help you in the process:

- Do you express yourself through your material possessions?
- Are you in work that motivates you or in work motivated by greed?
- Do you consider that possessions are as important as people?
- Does your interest in money / materialism prevent you from connecting with your family, friends and the wider community?
- Are you workaholic?
- Do you often compare what you own with what others own?
- Do your conversations normally centre on money / material goods or do you enjoy serious discussions and intellectual debates?
- Are you attached to the status which your job / profession gives you? E.g. Colonel Smith (Retired) or Mr. Smith (Inspector of Police-Retired).

If you have answered "yes" to most of the questions, then you have lost the consumer plot. You need to learn how to be detached a little more from material possessions which you are chasing.

Treat each new day as a gift. Anxiousness and envy for what is not, can give way to awareness and gratitude for what is.

The Five Senses

'The stormy senses drag the mind to the other side.'

(Bhagawad Gita)

Linked very closely to the Five Evil Passions are the five stormy senses which can pull us away from leading a more meaningful life or going through a spiritual experience. The five senses, usually reckoned, are the senses of sight, hearing, smell, taste and touch. Bhagat Ravidas in Guru Granth Sahib describes five different species that are destroyed by a weakness for one sense object. Then he observes that we can imagine the fate of human beings who have become slaves of all the five senses. He says: "The deer, fish. bumble bee, moth and elephant are doomed to destruction by one sense each, the deer by the smell of hearing, the fish by the sense of taste, the bumble bee by the sense of smell, the moth by the sense of sight and the elephant by the sense of touch. As we all know it happens as follows:

1. A deer is lured by sound. Attracted by the drumbeats it comes out into the open and gets shot.
2. A fish has weakness for taste. It bites the bait and gets killed.
3. A bee is attracted by smell. It enters the flower which closes in and destroys it.
4. A moth is attracted by sight. It dances around a flame and gets scorched to death.
5. An elephant falls for touch. During the mating season, the elephant gets restless and falls in the trap set by the hunters.

The five senses want physical pleasure, gratification, but if one is vigilant, one does not have to indulge in them. Humankind has been endowed with intellect. The senses are physical and do not affect the intellect. With mindfulness, your intellect can control the arousals induced by the senses. But if we follow the senses, we can be like a boat in water being pulled by the wind.

When you are seeking a truly meaningful life, you will be inspired by high values and principles. You will not be controlling the senses by merely denying yourself, but you will be substituting the baser desires with higher ones.

Overcoming the Evil Passions

"... Dispels his evils and shuns out the desires of his mind; who has full control over sexuality and is free from the five evils, such a person is the purest of the pure and is very rare."

(Guru Granth Sahib)

Subtle sensations occur all the time during our daily existence, so regularly that we can forget that they are there. These sensations change with our emotions and react in response to our circumstances and our internal talk or what we say to ourselves. Sometimes these sensations are painful, and sometimes pleasant. Unless we are fully aware of these sensations, we will react the same way to them, which means that we will be driven by negative vices like anger, greed, lust egoism etc. We will be battered by disappointments, seething with regret for things we should have done but not managed to do, or frustrated hopes. In other words, we will never change, but be the same usual self.

When you are self aware, attuned to that tranquillity within, you can be at peace in any environment. As Gandhi said, 'it is not difficult to find peace in peaceful circumstances. It needs extraordinary character and integrity to retain the peace in a disturbed environment.' The test is to try to maintain the balance when the environment is challenging. Human beings have the ability to attune to the inner peace within, away from the external noise and din.

Through a practice of conscious awareness of bodily sensations, whether pleasant or unpleasant, one can destroy old reaction patterns, and learns to react differently. When angry, we do not have to react the same way old way, we can be aware of the sensations and takes steps to calm down instead of responding in anger or violently. With mindfulness, you are calm with imperturbable equanimity, and this mental balance stands between you and the passions. It counteracts the rising anger or craving and aversion which overcome us from moment to moment. It will also reduce our suffering which we experience because of the way we feed the passions.

We can acknowledge human nature as it is, but be transformational and make it divine. Lust is channelled into love, and greed becomes the desire to create wealth, not just for oneself but for others. With such a transformation, we **can** "Make Poverty History."

According to the teachings of the Sikh Gurus, just as there are basic vices, there are five cardinal virtues. Each vice has one strong opposing virtue. Lust is overshadowed and defaced by self restraint (*sanjam*), anger by toleration, greed by contentment, worldly affection by devotion to duty. Self restraint is the golden principle.

Who controls his evil desires and frees himself from the five passions (Lust, anger, greed, false love, and ego)

O Nanak! Such a truly pure person is one in a million.

To be self aware, have a good look inside you.

Connecting with the Inner Body—Daily Practice

The aim of this activity is to encourage you to focus as intensively as possible on your immediate flow of awareness—on what you experience *here and now*.

- Make yourself comfortable and relax for a while, breathing slowly, steadily and deeply, but without effort.
- Let our mind focus on what ever you can see, hear, smell and taste.
- You might like to focus on each sensory perception in turn, or you may prefer to allow which ever sense dominates your attention at any one time to do so. Try to be aware of what you are experiencing e.g. I am aware of fresh air caressing my skin; I am aware of a noise like a car being started in the

neighbourhood. At the same time try to be aware of what the process of being consciously aware of focusing your attention in this feels like, i.e. does it give you a sense of aliveness or alertness?

- Direct your attention to the inner body. Feel it from within and focus on the feelings of your inner body when ever possible. You don't have to remove the focus from what ever you are doing; you can feel the inner body at the same time.
- When challenges come, as they always do in life, make it a habit to go within. Attention to your inner body does not mean that you are thinking about the emotion, it means just to observe the emotion, to acknowledge and accept it as it is. Some emotions are easily identified, anger, fear and grief and so on, others may be difficult to label. Probe for cues or signals such as feelings of psychological distress, internal verbalizations of the situation, anxiety, rising anger, depression, fear, physical distress—sweating, blushing, heart rate increase, butterflies in the stomach etc.
- This need not take long, just a few seconds, but you need to do it at the moment when a difficult situation arises. Any delay will allow the emotion to take over and the usual reaction will arise. When you are in touch with your inner body, you immediately still the mind and become 'present'. You are not following the dictates of the mind.
- If you are not aware, you will continue to be run by your mind. The script in your head, your disposition to act in certain ways, the conditioning of your mind will dictate your behaviour.
- Your will then be following the usual pattern, the conditioned reaction will then be involuntary, automatic and predictable.

A Buddhist saying sums up these points thus: **'Become the master of your mind rather than let your mind become your master.'**

Being Alert

One of my Karate masters, to test the degree of alertness or presence, would sneak from behind to attack us. He wanted his students to be in a state of alertness. The alert students would notice the sensei (teacher) creeping from behind and would stop him or step aside. Those who were caught were hit from behind—they were not alert, or were unconscious as to what was happening around them.

That was the training for external attacks, to be alert and to be on the look out for anybody sneaking on you. Have a good look inside you also. Are you carrying unspoken resentment toward a person close to you? Do you realise that the energy you thus emanate, the vibrations you give, are hurtful for you as well as those around you? In a fully conscious or attentive mind, an emotion has a very short life span. It's like a momentary ripple. However an emotion can survive inside you for days and weeks if you feed it, and can join with other emotions, and like a parasite can survive inside you for a long time. It feeds on your energy.

So when you are being attentive to the 'here and now' you are conscious of your behaviour, to your reactions, moods, and thoughts as they arise, in the present moment. You deal with the past on the level of the present, in the present moment. The more attention you give to a negative event of the past, the more you energize it, and the more likely you will identify with it. If you can be present enough to watch all that is happening inside you, in your mind, the factors that are affecting your moods, then you are alert. When you do not observe them critically, or analytically, but non- judgementally, then you are being mindful, being your conscious self. You are not going into the past, but coming into the present. Just like the students were not expected to chase their sensei after observing him sneaking upon them, but just to be aware, to know, when to step aside.

As you become more conscious of your present reality, you may get an insight into the ways you function, or how your conditioned mind reacts. In 'Anger Management Courses,' the participants realise why their relationships follow certain patterns, arguments escalate and become more and more emotional and even violent. The realization is helpful, and they want to change.

Your consciousness being in the present moment can be the transformative agent. Your conditioned mind cannot react in the same way, in your presence. You are alert, fully awake and can decide to respond in a different manner to a similar stimulus, or to put it more simply, to make a different choice in a similar situation.

Living in the Present (Here and Now)

A stanza of an ancient Indian poem entitled, 'Seize the day.' captures the importance of living in the present:

Look to this day! —

For Yesterday is but a dream,

And Tomorrow is only a vision:

But Today well lived makes,

Every Yesterday a dream of Happiness,

And every Tomorrow a Vision of Hope,

Look well therefore to this Day.

The past is already gone and the future has not yet come. We cannot live in the past, though we often talk about it. When people are sitting together, they often talk about their past, interesting anecdotes, where they have excelled, their childhood, their achievements etc. Some times it feels that people live in the past only.

Some people get depressed or angry when they talk about certain experiences, or incidents that happened to them. The answer lies in just being in the present. If you want to be a slave of your past, then it is fine, but if you want peace of mind, internal stillness, then you have to work to refrain from entertaining all the resentments, the perceived wrongs and all the depressive experiences. You have to find mechanisms to release yourself from a load of mental investments, and unload the baggage you carry all the time. You are not a victim of your past. You are in charge of the present moment.

You have to let go of thoughts and feelings as they arise or you will be recalling incidents that happened yesterday, last year and even a decade ago. You are not living in the present if you are thinking about what you did yesterday or what you will do next year.

A conscious person's main focus of attention is NOW, though they are peripherally aware of what happened in the past. If you made a mistake in the past, learn from it 'now.' On the other hand if you dwell on it mentally, you will find it hard to let it go, feelings of guilt, anger, shame etc. come up, then you are making the mistake of turning into 'me' and 'mine.' It becomes 'how stupid of me' rather than 'it was a mistake.' You are then, hard on yourself. You make it part of your sense of self, where as you are not your mistakes, guilt and self-criticism.

It is the quality of your consciousness at this moment that determines your future; otherwise the past will perpetuate itself through lack of presence. The same old patterns of thought followed by action, desires accompanied by frustrations, pain and suffering brought in by greed are acted out in repeat performances.

We believe that problems were caused by specific situations in life and that is true only up to a certain degree. If all your problems and their perceived causes were miraculously removed, but you had not become more mindful, more conscious, living more in the present, you would find your self with the same set of problems. It would be just like people who have managed to shed lot of pounds in body weight only to put it back after a few months, because there is no **real** change in the lifestyle.

The mind will be functioning or dysfunctioning as before and we will be reacting in the same way in similar situations. The response to a similar stimulus will be the same. There will be no pause to consider the consequences of the actions. The best indicator of mindfulness is how you deal with life's challenges when they come. Through these challenges, you can become more intensely conscious. You learn to be mindful or witness to your thoughts and emotions, which are an essential part of being present rather than letting intense negativity such as anger, fear, aggression, depression and so on, take over. On the level of your thinking, you will be aware of your discontent, and the form of judgement which is leading to unease in the body. On the emotional level, there will be an undercurrent of unease, tension or nervousness.

People often feel that they did not get this or that when they were young. We may have been deprived of material things, or even love as a child, but we cannot go back. Just try accepting things as they are, and give up blaming others or your self. List your assets, your treasures and your talents, that are **you.** Think of what you have now rather than pondering on about what you did not have.

Nothing that has happened in the past can prevent you from being what you want to be. A research by the University Of New England, New South Wales studied 219 sets of twins to determine the influence of genes in our life. Dr. J. Malouff its author said that genes have a bigger influence on our lives than thought, but 'genes are not destiny. They are a powerful force, so we have to put a substantial amount of effort into changing things that are ingrained.' Nature Versus Nurture is an age old argument and still there is no clear winner.

Freeing yourself from the Past

A new action

Think of something you would like to do but would not ordinarily do, e.g. speaking to someone you would like to know, giving a present to someone, climbing Mt. Kilimanjaro.

- Imagine or visualize yourself doing it.
- Do it. Carry out the action you have created and visualized.
- Be aware that you have chosen to do it, and have carried out an action which otherwise would not happened.

A new you

Gradually widen the scope of this exercise. Try behaving towards others, for example, in a way that you would like to but have not done so far. Try setting events in train which you would like to happen but have not bothered, hoped or dared to bring about.

Thoughts

"What we are today comes from our thoughts of yesterday, and our present thoughts build our life of tomorrow: our life is the creation of the mind". Most people take the view that they cannot control their deliberate thought processes, they have a hold on them. They try to let them go, but the thoughts have a life of their own. We need to remember that, 'my thoughts are my thoughts, and no body is controlling them. The thoughts are not above me or beyond me.' If you are honest with yourself, and with critical thinking you can discern why you loathe letting them go or can't control them. The difficulty in letting go of negative thoughts usually arises because we are attached to them, we cultivate them. We believe them, we enjoy thinking them, and they are normally centred on others.

A thought is a wonderful attribute of the human mind. If we want to live in the present moment, there is no point in a thought that dwells on an event in the past. Anything that happened last year, last month, and last week or even in the last hour is in the past. It is just that we need to learn how to use it. Thoughts are creations of the mind passing through. Be aware of them and use them to your advantage. When you listen to your thoughts, detect the point at which they start to drift, and bring yourself back by coming to the present moment.

We cannot prevent thoughts from arising. A new thought arises every nanosecond. They arise because you have a normal properly functioning mind. In Punjabi, the mind is called *chenchal* which means never still, always on the move. It will travel in all the four directions if you are unconscious or unmindful of what it is up to. But a thought that arises spontaneously is just a thought, you can simply let go of it. You don't have to follow it. It can't be classified as 'right' or 'wrong', what you do is important.

Spontaneous thoughts come all the time, so if possible, try to have the right relationship with your thoughts, let them come and pass. We do not have to hold on to them or cultivate them. The deliberate thoughts are the ones we need to be careful of and set them aside. Even if you look at the spontaneous thoughts seriously, you will recognise that more thoughts are deliberate than at first seemed to be the case. Deliberate thoughts are the ones you bring into consciousness again and again, to meditate on and probably act on. If the deliberate thoughts are negative, it is crucial that you gain control over them, otherwise they will guide your actions. You will be a slave of your negative thoughts and can never be internally still.

The ability to think things through is vital to our well being, but if that faculty never stops, keeps entertaining the same thoughts, then we are the slave of our thinking rather than its master. And, we have a problem! The world we experience is the world created within our minds, with our thoughts. Our thoughts and feelings depend upon how we view the world, but they are not absolutes which cannot be changed. By learning not to be driven by our negative thoughts and feelings, we can see how emancipating it is. Regardless of religious standpoint; Good and Evil do exist, but almost all in human mind. Most of us want to be 'good' and recognise our true nature. We want to change and make the world a better place. By doing something about our negative and sometimes even abhorrent thoughts, we are directly reducing the amount of evil spread in the world. More attention to our inner heart will benefit society. The problem is that we often muffle the voice of our spirit instead of putting a muffler on our negative thoughts.

Changing Thoughts and Feelings

How to do it

Look around and write, 'I am thinking— '(write down what you are thinking at that very moment), and 'I am feeling....' (Write down a single word to describe the emotion). Perform this activity for about 10 minutes. Notice how many times you can change your feelings in 10 minutes. Repeat the exercise and try to increase the number of positive feelings you can experience in 10 minutes. You can choose to notice what you want to notice, and ignore what you do not want to observe or look at, or listen to. This increases the chance that you can find something positive to think about, and in the process feel better.

Progression: Now observe your inner body, the feelings and the thoughts that are being generated. Notice the emotion and bad feelings, and check whether your mind is holding on to a grievance pattern such as blame, resentment that is feeding the emotion. This will indicate that you have a problem or a challenge to be faced. Use these feelings as *signals* to begin the process of problem solving, and self management rather than as *triggers* that set off self destructive activity by giving into afflictive emotions.

Re-Framing: Devise positive alternative explanations for situations or thoughts in which negative definitions lead to the likelihood of losing temper or your cool. A nagging partner can be re-framed as someone who really cares. Hostility from someone can be re-framed as an opportunity for using self-control strategies.

Thought- Stopping: You can put an end to patterns of repetitive negative thoughts, by commanding them to "stop." 'That is enough.' They will cease at once. When they return seconds later, simply repeat "stop" again and you will feel clarity and stillness in the moments waiting for the next thought. If nothing else happens, initially at least, you will not be feeding the negative thoughts which lead to negative feelings. During the 'waiting' time, try to be present in the present moment, in your present life. Gradually, you will become more rooted in yourself, and not thinking or anticipating your next move. You will become totally involved in what is happening to you now. This sensation is subtle yet wonderful, and once you have experienced it, you will likely want to create it again and again and not indulge in negative thoughts or obsessions about people.

Witness Stance: Mentally stand back and observe all your thoughts and include the beliefs as well. You can learn to say, 'Ah! Look, I am torturing myself today,' or 'Ah! Look, I am being kind to myself today.' We can thus dissociate from our thoughts or, believe them. Through developing the witness position, we can realize that we are not our thoughts or our feelings, and can get a bit of distance.

Mindfulness

Mindfulness improves our ability to maintain an inner calmness in stressful situations, as there is a development of personal stability in the context of challenges and tribulations. With mindfulness we have deeper clarity of thinking, improved communication in the sense that we listen attentively and try to understand the people we are interacting with. Mindfulness helps us to develop better decision making, as you think through creatively before acting, and to accept others as fellow human beings.

When meditating, just meditate, when praying, just pray, when working, just work, and when playing a sport, just play. In other words, keeping your mind with what you are doing is the key. This is often referred to as 'being mindful', and we can train ourselves to be mindful. Mindfulness can gradually encompass all your activities. When you have reasoned that something is worth doing, then it is better that you put your whole being into it, and if with mindfulness you decide that it is not a good thing to do, then don't do it.

I find that the practice of meditating can be applied to other activities as well. The mind will wander when reciting the prayers, you try to keep it centred on the prayer, or the mantra, and in case of meditation on the breath or what ever you are meditating on. Similarly, when doing any activity, when the mind wanders, bring it back to the task in hand. When you notice that your mind is wandering, you have already won half the battle. Don't be angry with yourself or be harsh on yourself, which only makes matters worse. Try to be present in the present moment and let go of what ever is being brought in by your ego or mind.

With mindfulness, you will be aware of negative emotions, so don't feed them, or entertain them and they will gradually disappear. We don't have to seek enjoyment at the uninvited expense of others. If you have limiting beliefs, like, I can't do it, or 'I am too old for this' challenge them and recognise them as limiting beliefs only and not facts. The most important thing is to bring back your mind to the job in hand.

Mindfulness should increase our ability to enjoy what ever opportunities life presents. As your mindfulness develops, you might find that your thinking becomes clearer and more focused. As said earlier, there is clarity of Thinking and Communication. When you are focused, you are also confident and exude self esteem.

Meditation and Mindfulness

A study carried out by Mood Disorders Centre at the University of Exeter in 2008 found that meditation is as effective as drugs at combating depression. Psychologists from the University into mindfulness based cognitive therapy (MBCT); find it to be better than drugs or counselling. The MBCT technique revolves around mindfulness meditation. Mindfulness meditation can help prevent the 'downward spiral' of thoughts that often brings about depression. In this, you sit with your eyes closed and focus on your breathing. Concentrating on the rhythm of the breath helps to produce a feeling of detachment. The idea is that you come to realize that thoughts come and go of their own accord and that your conscious self is distinct from your thoughts.

One reason given by experts for depression is that sadness can turn into obsessive brooding. When you live in the present, you do not brood over the sad times. Living in the present is said to help people focus on the 'Now' instead of dwelling on the past or planning the future. Instead of brooding, you are focussed on what ever you are doing now, and are compassionate to your self and others. It could shorten lists for psychological therapies.

Nature

We are too often caught up in the drama of the day; our pain, stress at workplace, the demands of family, financial problems and so on. We forget that 'I am alive, and have a life and some purpose to it. We often do not realize that it is the most basic things that bring us the greatest joy because they are so much with us. We need to remind ourselves that we have fire, water and earth and that these elements should be celebrated. There are places in Africa where there is hardly any clean water available. A mother has to travel eight miles to fetch water in a bucket to wash her children and cook food. The water is not clean and the children are often sick with dysentery and other ailments.

All of us living in advanced countries have water, and I hope that every body drinks a few litres every day. We enjoy a variety of things like tea, coffee, lassie (buttermilk), juice and a whole lot more. But how often do we appreciate the miracle that is the liquid we drink. Without a steady supply of water we would live only a few days. Water makes up 60-70% of the human body. People cannot survive more than five or six days without water or two or three days in a hot environment. Water also coves 70% of the earth's surface and occurs as standing (oceans, lakes) and running (rivers, streams) water, rain and vapour and supports all forms of life on Earth. Most of the water is in the sea, less than 0.01 is fresh water.

Scientists predict that future geo-politics will be about water. Without a steady supply of water we could live only a few days. Having access to water is really a reason to be joyful and thankful to Nature. We thank the waiter who brings us a cup of tea, or some body who fetches us a glass of water when we are thirsty, but forget the 'Creator' who has made water available in such abundance, and free of charge.

So next time you drink water, notice something about the water as you swallow a sip. Feel it within you, feel the water's presence. As you take more sips, notice its relationship with you. Think of the lakes and rivers you have seen, or if it comes from a well, then think of the deep or the shallow well. Think of nature that has made an abundant supply of the water and appreciate that you have it in abundance. Most of us take the supply of water. for granted and fail to appreciate simple things in life. Maybe this is the time to be grateful, and celebrate one of the most important things on earth.

Some religions have called 'Earth' the great mother. If we take earth as our mother, then so far we have not been very good sons and daughters of the earth. We are good at plundering the planet for our own immediate ends and living in a way that is fatal for the next generation and the ones to follow but do not know how to enjoy nature. A walk near the sea side can be a joy, and refreshing when you feel the warm sun on your skin and the gentle breeze caressing you.

Scientists at the University of Glasgow recently found that using parks and playing fields for walks and other activities lowers blood pressure and cuts the harmful effects of stress.

'Getting in touch with nature is a great strategy for relaxation. Modern life is inuring us to the comforts of life and we are forgetting how to reach the wide open spaces, the woods and the beaches. Nature is quite beautiful to the eye. Nature's gifts abound, being one with nature can influence your mood for the better. If you are feeling low, go for a leisurely walk in the fresh air. As you are walking appreciate the beauty created by nature, the shape of the trees, their height, the colour, shape and texture of the leaves. If you are living in the city, your local park could help you to reconnect with nature. Whilst there, you can examine the various species of plants. Some councils spend large amounts of money on improving and maintaining their parks.

Happiness and Unhappiness

There is only one cause of unhappiness: the false belief you have in your head, beliefs so widespread, so commonly held, that it never occurs for you to question them.

(Anthony de Mello)

The fact that there is always a positive side to life is the one thing that gives me a lot of happiness. This world is not perfect. There are problems. But things like happiness and unhappiness are relative. Realizing this gives you hope.

(Dalai Lama)

Jeremy Bentham (1748-1832) is best known as one of the founding fathers of an ethical system called **utilitarianism**. Bentham says that 'Nature has placed mankind under the governance of two sovereign masters, pain and pleasure. Utilitarianism does not take the selfish view that we some times adopt that it is just my own happiness that matters. Every one's happiness is to count equally. Our aim, according to Bentham should be to promote *the greatest happiness of the greatest number*. As Bentham himself puts it, 'the greatest happiness of the greatest number is the foundation of morals and legislation.

Most of us ordinary mortals want happiness but do not want to contemplate unhappiness. Utilitarianism insists that happiness is what we ought to aim for. But is happiness really something we should value most? We need to remind ourselves that somebody may enjoy eating chicken, but if the same dish is served every day, for breakfast, lunch and dinner, the person will get fed up. I remember once when climbing Mt. Kilimanjaro, I ate tinned beans for three days. On the fourth day, I wanted anything else but beans. I thought I reeked of beans.

Bhagat Kabir (1518) was an Indian saint-poet[1].is said to have prayed to God that he doesn't want happiness. Happiness brings unhappiness in its wake just like darkness follows sunlight, and birth ultimately is followed by death. Kabir's belief is very similar to Gautama Buddha's philosophy which involves a theory about the nature of human existence and how we might achieve release from suffering. Buddha believed that life is suffering. We see pain, frustration and misery all around us. Our suffering, which is, both physical and mental may be punctuated by brief moments of happiness, but the suffering soon returns.

Another devotee of God, Namdev, and a saint poet from Maharashtra (India) said that he welcomes happiness and unhappiness, pleasure and pain equally, but asks God to help him retain his equilibrium in both happy and unhappy circumstances.

Let us take another example to explain the diminishing of happiness. At a concert a singer sings a song beautifully and the public loves it. But if the singer decider to sing it again, she would probably get half the applause. If the singer decides to sing it for the third time, the public would grunt and groan to show their disapproval. If the singer has the audacity to sing for the fourth time, most of the audience would leave the concert. The lyrics may be elegant, the vocal music enthralling, but it is the repetition which has taken the joy out of the concert.

Hedonism is the pursuit of pleasure; it's sensual self indulgence. The psychological version of hedonism holds that human actions are motivated primarily by a search for pleasure and the avoidance of pain. Now let us suppose that a new machine is built—let us call it a pleasure machine. The device can simulate or replicate any experience of your choice, to enjoy a romantic evening with a person you have always fancied, to converse with a world leader of your choice or any one of your icons. Those who enjoy what John Mills calls 'higher pleasures' can enjoy cerebral activities—those of thought, feeling and imagination. Those who enjoy the 'lower pleasure' can enjoy sensuous or physical attractions. His son John Stuart Mill insisted that some pleasures were of greater value than others. He famously wrote that, 'it is better to be a human being dissatisfied than a pig satisfied; better to be a Socrates dissatisfied than a fool satisfied.' Thus Mill distinguishes between higher and lower pleasures.' and refines views advanced by both his father and Bentham.

Many of us would jump at the opportunity of trying the pleasure machine for a day or two, but no body would like to be permanently attached to such a device. And if it were done, it would become boring, tiresome and pleasure would turn into pain. A computer generated happiness might appeal to some, but most of us want to have a purpose and meaning in life, to live a life that is authentic and not live in a virtual world.

Quite often, this is something which happens on our 'dream holidays'. We love the place we have gone to for a few days but then the lustre starts wearing off, and we start thinking of returning—coming back to our 'sweet home'. Even animals after grazing in the lush green field during the day, like to come back to their sheds (home) in the evening.

Quite often unhappiness lies in the gap between our expectations and reality. A study about happiness found that Finnish mothers isolated by dark winters, were actually happier than Italian mothers with big families. The reason was that in Finland, everybody knows that winter travel is difficult, and you don't expect to see your children. But in Italy, where big, cheerful families are the norm, a missed visit by the children is a catastrophe.

So if you feel unhappy, it may be worth asking yourself:

- What would make me happy?
- Are my expectations realistic?
- **If they are not realistic, try to explore how to make them realistic. Be honest about your expectations and work on them rather than blaming the other party who is not meeting your expectations.**

I suppose that happiness is important in our lives, but it is not the only thing of importance.

Stoicism to Overcome Evil Passions

I – smile a hard set smile, like a stoic and let the world have its way. (Tennyson)

Stoicism was a Greek school of philosophy and in the 3rd and 2nd century's stoics took a prominent part in Greek and Roman revolutionary movements. After the 1st century BC stoicism became the philosophy of the ruling Roman ruling class and lost its revolutionary significance. However, such was Stoicism's impact on the Greek and Roman world that it has left its mark on the language we use today—when we describe as stoical or 'philosophical' an attitude of self disciplined , uncomplaining and courageous acceptance of all that life brings . Stoicism had appealed to some of the best and most intelligent minds of the ancient world.

It is a philosophy which enjoins self mastery and the courage to treat both good and ill fortune as irrelevant to true inner stability of our heart. The stoic philosophy was primarily concerned with living in accordance with one's own nature and Universal Nature.

Self education in stoic living is to be effected by emulating an ideal wise man—even if such a sage exists only in imagination, and even if one cannot attain that state of moral perfection. The endeavour is the important thing, and the goal is to live in agreement with nature, in the sense of living in conformity with the rational order of things, thereby achieving peace and strength of mind.

The central tenet of Epictetus's teaching was that we must distinguish between what lies within our power and what lies outside our power, learning how to master the former and to accept the latter with fortitude. Only our emotions, thoughts and appetites—our inner mental life are in our power, so we must govern these while cultivating stoic indifference to factors beyond our control. These latter include not only what the world and other people do to us, but some of the ungovernable factors like acts of nature.

The philosophy is quite similar to the Prayer of Serenity which is:

God grant me the serenity to accept the things I cannot change,

Courage to change the things I can,

And wisdom to know the difference.

Amen

Stoics regarded the passions as natural and said that the way to deal with them properly is to master them by understanding them. Consider the example of fear, reason dictates that we are courageous in the face of danger, but fear does not obey, and makes one run away. Fight and flight are two natural instincts inherited from our ancestors, which helped them in their survival in harsh conditions. Stoicism says that by understanding the true nature of fear, and bringing it under control of self discipline, one turns it into something positive. It is transformed into carefulness or appropriate caution. In this way the other passions can be converted into what the Stoics call good feelings, among them kindness, generosity and amity.

Plato argued that an ideal city state is one in which each of the community's three orders of citizens—the governors, the guardians or military men and the general population—do what is appropriate for their position in society, and thereby preserve a balance or social harmony between them. Then Plato draws his analogy between the state and the individual. Just as the city has three components, so an individual soul has three parts, reason, the emotions and the appetites. Where these are in harmony, the individual is happy.

Journey of Self Discovery

One who remains unaffected by weal or woe, by covetousness, by worldly love and ego,

Is the Image of God, hear this O man! says Nanak

(Guru Granth Sahib)

It's a journey to discover your own battles against the five evil vices—lust, excessive anger, covetousness, worldly love, and ego. If you succeed, it's a victory over the inner battles. The challenge comes from within your self; it doesn't come from outside, the opponent is one's self. It's an endeavour to develop your inner strength, to discover the magic potency of self-governance. It enriches you from within. The reward is deeply personal and private. You create a new level of awareness. Carl Jung said, "Who looks outside dreams, who looks inside awakes."

With true commitment, setbacks are seen as learning opportunities. People with low commitment often see the setbacks as justification to abandon self growth and development. You are aware of your purpose in life and are trying to give meaning to life. Persistence through many setbacks and obstacles will pay dividends. If you persevere you will be enriched by the experience of trying. It will be internal success rather than worldly success.

A river eventually finds its way to the sea, its final destination. Its goal is to merge with the sea, and to achieve it, has twists and turns, it meanders, changes its speed and direction, and finally reaches its destination. A river flows along the 'line of least resistance. Relax and enjoy the process, appreciate that the journey will lead to deep understanding, development and maturity.

Footnotes

1 Bhagat is an honorary title meaning 'devotee'.

[illegible]

[illegible] finally finds its way to the sea, its final destination. Its goal is to merge with the sea, and to achieve it, it has to [illegible] and turns [illegible] to speed and direction, and [illegible] along the lines of least [illegible]

Chapter 4

Is There a Purpose to Life?

You are here to enable the divine purpose of the universe to unfold. That is how important you are!

Eckhart Tolle

Most of us live the same type of life irrespective of background or ethnicity. We spend our youth being educated. Then we find a job in accordance with our education or the skills acquired. We meet someone, marry and have children. We buy a house, try to make a success of our business, or our career, and aim for a bigger house or a better car. We go on holidays with our family and friends, and talk about it till the next holiday. The biggest dilemmas some of us ever have to face are where to take our next holiday or whom to invite for our next party. We plan for our retirement but worry that our pension or savings may not be enough. Some wise people indicate that our lives are petty and repetitive, wasted in the pursuit of the trivial, because we seem to know of nothing better. Most of us think that our life is fine if we have a dream house, but others may consider that a life in pursuit of materialism only is hollow and futile.

People often wonder, 'Who Am I?' In serious discussions or discourses what comes across is the quest to know, 'What should I be doing with my life?' or if they feel that they are not leading useful lives, then they wonder where they went wrong. People have lost an essential sense of self. When people ask themselves such questions or discuss with others, they are seeking a purpose and meaning in life.

Sooner or later everybody wonders whether there is a meaning and purpose to life. When contemplating about our place in the universe, we are little further along than when time began. We are still left with the questions of who we are, why we are here and where we are going. People get disaffected with the way things are in their lives, and seek a meaning in their lives. "I have been asking why I'm here most of my life?" often comes up in serious discussions or discourses. Elie Wiesel, a survivor of the Nazi death camps observed, "Why are we here? is the most important question a human being has to face...I believe that life has a meaning, in spite of the meaningless deaths I have seen."

Is it important to find out if life has a meaning, if there is a purpose to life? Victor Frankl[1] Mental health professional and author of, *The Ultimate Meaning in Life* says, "The striving to find a meaning in one's life is the primary motivational force in man...There is nothing in the world, I venture to say, that would so effectively help one to survive even the worst conditions, as the knowledge that there is a meaning in one's life."

Is life just to work hard, to improve our living conditions, to provide for our families and then go to another world? It must be admitted that some doubt if there is purpose to life. Most of the young people have this aspiration—to have a spouse, have children, a house, perhaps a car as well, and be happy. Are we here just to complete our tenure on this earth and after sixty or seventy years, cease our existence for ever?

Many people in the world, that is in Eastern and Western lands feel that the main purpose in life is to acquire wealth. They believe that material wealth can lead to a happy and meaningful life. But what do the people who have wealth say about it. Harry Bruce, a Canadian writer says:" A baffling number of people insist that they are not happy." Former U S president Jimmy Carter expressed his view thus: "We have discovered that owning things does not satisfy our longing for meaning...Piling up material goods cannot fill the emptiness of lives which have no confidence or purpose." Research carried out by the British Government in 2008 showed that people might have grown richer, but over the past 50years there has been no associated increase in happiness. (The research was carried out before the banking crises and down turn in the economy). We are actually more prone to mental illness—10 times more people suffer from depression than in 1945.

Many psychiatrists believe that a tendency to medicate depression out of existence is a mistake. Here we are not talking of severe immobilizing depression in which one's thoughts are rarely far from suicide, when every thing is very bleak, no past to be proud of, the present circumstances are seen as unpleasant with no future to look forward to—but rather general feelings of gloom.

Professor J. Wakefield of New York University has co-authored a book entitled, *The Loss of Sadness: How psychiatry transformed normal sorrow into depressive disorder*. He believes that the emotion of sadness has evolved for good reasons, such as compelling us to suspend our normal functioning for a certain period of reflection. We can learn some lessons through reflection. A cautious approach or wariness of future sadness can also prevent us from repeating past mistakes.

Mild depression can simply be a strong signal that something fundamental in one's life needs to change. Preventing oneself chemically from feeling 'the spur of sadness' at all is avoiding reality, recognising things as they are, and removing the veil of delusion. In the1950's a drugs company Geigy made the first 'happy pill' called Imipramine. The company were reluctant to spend money to promote the pill as it was felt that the number of people with endogenous depression or melancholia who might benefit was too small. Since then the range of people for whom medication is considered appropriate has extended as far as those whose only symptoms are, "crying or feeling sorry for themselves."

Dr James LeFanu, author of many books and correspondent for The Daily and Sunday Telegraph says that, "This explains the common observation that while some do indeed benefit from Prozac and similar anti depressant drugs, the majority of those to whom they are prescribed do not."

Alastair Sandhurst explains in the British Medical Journal that many are not suffering from depression, they feel sad, pessimistic, hopeless, but closer questioning reveals that their real problem is the absence of a purpose to their lives, of higher goals or aspirations. Prozac may work wonders fore melancholia but regrettably it cannot imbue a sense of purpose into those who believe their lives are pointless.

A person with higher values understands that there are more important things to aspire to than be absorbed in the gratification of the senses only. Such a person is aware of their desire to move to a higher spiritual plane or observe the high values espoused at all times. It may require a major shift in attitude and behaviour, to move from lower level values to higher level values. A person with high values will realize that happiness does not lie in external things, It lies within with the realization that you are true to yourself and live in accordance with the high ideals.

Even your job can give you meaning and purpose in life. You need to ask yourself, 'Are you working for money only?' or, 'Are you dedicating your work to a higher cause?' Develop the right attitude to your job and the most mundane work becomes a source of joy. Your job becomes your vocation and the vocation becomes a service. With such an attitude to work, you will be constructing a secure base within yourself, and stepping on the path to spirituality. You will be earning money for your needs, for your sustenance, but have a meaning and purpose to your life. The real purpose of your existence will be to be of service to others. This will also give a meaning to your life, as you try to serve others with a smile, with pleasure, being useful to others.

People who do not have enough or regular income will be focussing on getting the next meal. It is difficult to take the inward journey when the stomach is empty. Once you have food and shelter, you can focus on discovering the purpose and meaning to your life. The spiritual journey can begin when basic needs such as shelter; sustenance and security have been met. Without a roof over the head, or a secure place, and food in the kitchen any higher purpose is difficult to achieve or focus on.

Self Realization

Self realization is about fulfilment of one's potential, finding out what you are looking for in your life? It is a step towards spirituality; some of the questions you may wish to reflect on are:

- Who AM I?
- What is the True purpose of my life?
- Does life really have a meaning?
- What do I want from my life and from the meaning /purpose in life?
- Do I really want to change or am I happy with the way things are?
- Where am I now? (With regard to Real meaning and True purpose in life).
- Where do I want to be?
- How can I achieve what I want to be or self realization?

Descartes holds that since God created him, it is probable that he has placed his image and similitude upon him.

When we realize our true nature, we realize our essence, and we realize compassion. Compassion manifests as the wish to help all beings. To understand this wish, is to know the purpose of life, what is really important in life, and then the practical question of 'how to live' is no longer addressed from the point of, **'what do**

I want?' but from the perspective of–what is it that is good to do? After meditating on what is good to do, we can move on to— **how to do good**

'Good' is that which helps beings. Each person has to discover how to manifest compassion in his or her life. The principles are the same for every one, but the specifics will depend upon each person's circumstances and abilities. No progress can be made unless we are willing to let go of selfish desires. It is important that we have faith in the purity of our essential being, as we shall have to trust ourselves both in order to reflect deeply and act to serve other beings.

Some where along the way, we seem to have forgotten what is we really want in excessive consumerism and materialism. We get sucked up in hedonism (which is the natural pleasure principle) and believe that the satisfaction of our desires is the ultimate aim of human life. It's stock taking time of your life if you do not feel that you are being yourself, you are rushing through life without contemplating about your true nature. We all need to find a distinction between the material needs of survival and the way to a more meaningful life.

Rather than concentrating on our quest for money only, it is worthwhile looking at the big picture—of self fulfilment and the need to create a life with meaning. If you feel that self fulfilment is lacking, you can **change.** Most of us get caught up in greed and consumerism. You can have a life that you want, that is in accordance with your values, with a meaning rather than pursuing the same old lifestyle. We can learn new patterns of behaviour, depending upon how we explain it to ourselves. Change will happen if you have a clear vision which is underpinned by values, principles and targets. To flex the mind is better than being rigid.

The change will happen because it is what you want; it is what you have chosen. You can make a life that works rather than a life that works you. You cannot control whether other people are authentic, but you can decide whether or not you will be. With self realization, awareness of your values and beliefs, you become like a deeply rooted tree that can stand the strongest wind.

Top Tips

- Allow the space in your heart and mind to be open to new possibilities and new visions.
- Know you are preparing yourself for new adventure and a new life-with a real meaning and true purpose.
- Begin looking forward to a new you with trust and anticipation –knowing and trusting that you will receive and be blessed by a Higher Power. God helps those who help themselves. If you don't believe in God, trust yourself.
- Know that you are safe because you are not pursuing a trivial desire, but trying to realise your real potential, your ideal. Observe the process of change.
- It is fine to let go of the past. You are not programmed to do the same things.

We are often reluctant to answer and follow the call to our purpose, because we think that doing so may lead to major changes in our lifestyle. Nick Williams asserts that 'like iron fillings around a magnet, our life will form around the purpose. There may be disruption for a while as our life is rearranged to be more true and more supportive of our purpose. Our purpose has always been there, like an invisible path that we may see out of the corner of our eye but never really focus on.'

You are putting a moral intent in the forefront, a moral compass that will guide you in the world around you. Your intent and strong belief in the real meaning and true purpose you believe in will begin to change your reality. The more you try to support yourself and endeavour to live according to your beliefs and values, the more people around you will support you. If they don't, it will not bother you, because of your firm beliefs, and the knowledge that you are on the right track.

More Meaningful Life

Each of us possesses an exquisite, extraordinary gift; the opportunity to give expression to Divinity on earth through our every day lives. When we choose to honour the priceless gift, we participate in the recreation of the world.

(Sarah Ban Breathnach—Author of *Simple Abundance*)

I am not ruling out completely that people who are leading a hand to mouth existence cannot achieve great heights. Kabir a well known sage in India who still has a large following, was not well off financially and his mother used to admonish him to work hard to alleviate their poverty, but Kabir indicated that if he put all his attention in his work, he would not be able to remember God or recite His name. But Kabir once addressed God thus: 'Take your rosary. You can't worship on an empty stomach. 'St Francis of Assisi, a Christian ascetic was the son of a wealthy textile merchant. He began to devote himself to the care of lepers, whom he had formerly found repellent and renounced or gave up his right to inherit his father's property, returning even his clothes to his father. A simple life allows us to think or to meditate and "to get away from it all."

Embracing poverty, which he spoke of as his bride, he acquired his food by begging.

Gautama Buddha slipped outside the palace walls to experience life for himself. For the first time he saw a sick person, an old person and a dead person. Deeply troubled by the suffering of sickness, ageing and death, he came to the conclusion that the everyday mundane life was without substance. Later, inspired by some religious practitioners, Buddha became captivated by the possibility of a higher, meaningful, spiritual life. At that point he escaped from the palace, leaving his princely life behind to pursue this vision.

Since then, Buddhism has been captivated by the possibility of a higher more meaningful spiritual life. Buddhists are encouraged to reflect on Gautama Buddha's life and in the process they begin to become concerned abut cyclic existence. For Buddhists, the repeated round of birth, ageing, sickness and death is cyclic existence or *samsara*. This is achieved by turning away from temporary distractions. Influenced by this attitude, monks take up a system of morality by taking vows of pure behaviour through seeking to avoid the ten non virtues.

Non virtues according to the Dalai Lama in, *How to Practise—The Way To a Meaningful Life*, are organised into three categories. The physical non virtues are: killing, stealing and sexual misconduct. The verbal non virtues are: lying, and divisive talk, and senseless chatter. The mental non virtues are: covetousness, harmful intent and wrong views.

Mahavira's story is also similar. Jains look upon Mahavira (Sanskrit, *maha*—great, *vira*—hero) as the greatest of their teachers, who preached and demonstrated the way to salvation, laying stress on the 'pure unchanging eternal law,' that all things living, all things breathing, all things what ever, should not be slain or treated with violence or assaulted or driven away.' Historians say that Mahavira was born in a very rich family. Mahavira renounced family life at the age of 30 to become a wandering ascetic. 'After twelve years of sever fasting to cleanse his body, silence to improve his speech and of meditation to clear his mind, he gained omniscience.' In general, Jain spiritual life rests on three commitments known as the Three Jewels. They are:

- Right Belief
- Right Knowledge
- Right Conduct

In Sikhism similar ideas are postulated but with a clear emphasis on—'purpose of this life.'

You have obtained the human body for a purpose.

This is your opportunity to meet the Lord of this world

(Guru Granth Sahib)

To achieve unity with God, one has to use the body, mind and soul. The virtuous action of the body is the service of others. Instead of keeping an eye on the wealth of others, one should labour for one's requirements and should also give something in charity. The help rendered to others should be without any desire for remuneration. Charity without any expectation of reward is a virtuous action. The foremost aim of an ideal Sikh is the service of humanity. "Work hard and share your earnings, Nanak, though shall find the way." (Guru Granth Sahib)

Nam japo, kirat karo, wand shako—To meditate on the True Name with understanding, to earn through honest and creative work –and share earnings with others –is the hallmark of Sikhism.

Nam Japo: The recitation of the prayers with mind and soul is an act of faith. The sayings of the sages inspire us to higher ideals and nobler acts, thus paving the way for our spiritual enlightenment. A belief in God, helps to look at the whole of humanity as one, and promotes a sense of responsibility to others.

God is One, yet He can be seen in innumerable forms created by Him[2].

(Guru Granth Sahib)

People have asked since times immemorial, questions that still trouble us today, both practical questions about how to live, how to be contented and transcendental questions such as:

- What is the meaning of life?
- What am I here on Earth here for?
- Why is there so much suffering in the world?
- Is there a God?

Who Am I?

True luxury is being able to find the time to sit and think about who we really are, where we have come from and where we are heading.

(From, *Reincarnation—Remarkable Stories of People Who Recall Past Lives)*

People often wonder 'Who AM I'? People have lost an essential sense of 'self'. What comes across is their desire to know and some times an assurance that they are leading useful lives. When people think about their life seriously, they are on the brink of a great quest for purpose and meaning in life. Some of the questions they might be asking are:

- What do you want from your life and from the meaning / purpose in your life?
- Where are you now and—where do you want to be?
- What should I be doing with my life to bring about the change?

I can't answer the question, 'Who am I'?—for you, but can say that you are not your education, your personal past, expectations of the family, or your programming. You are not your acts, for you are much bigger than a few actions here and there. You are not your successes and you are not your failures. Some people define themselves by their successes and minimise their failures, but successes and failures are just two sides of a coin. A failure can be turned into a success, and quite often people lose when they were almost near to a successful outcome or result.

Your search for purpose and meaning in life will give you direction and control over what you are and where you go in life. Once you are clear about your purpose in life, your mind will be focused on fulfilling the goal or higher ideals of your life. The awareness will make it crystal clear to you that you're being successful and facing setbacks has nothing to do with your self worth as a human being. People are not successful at everything they attempt and those who are initially very successful have not learned to handle failure.

Some suggestions to search for real meaning and purpose in life are:

- Define your ultimate meaning in writing as clearly as you can.
- If it is to be more human and recognise humanity in every one, write it down in your own words. This will make you aware of, 'what you want to be'.
- Begin to imagine what kind of difference the progress towards what will bring meaning and purpose in your life will bring to your life.
- What will it feel like and look like when you are on the path to following your real purpose and meaning in life.
- What will it look like and feel like when you have realized your higher goal?
- They say that time changes things, **but you actually have to change them yourself.** (Andy Warhol)

Being willing to transcend yourself will lead to self realization—because you are more than aware as to where you are now –and where you want to be. **Be the change you want to see in the world**. (Mahatma Gandhi)

Embedding Change

The curious paradox is that when I accept myself just as I am, then I can change.

(Carl Rogers)

Sometimes if you want to see a change for the better, you have to take things in your own hands.

(Clint Eastwood—when he stood for election as Mayor of Carmel).

When one starts thinking of changing, it can be anything, attitude, behaviour, lifestyle, and there will be resistance. It is not easy to change even though we accept that the world is changing all the time. We do not want to get out of our comfort zone. There can be denial that you have 'wrong habits,' and even anger if some one else points them out. Initially there may be a guarded acceptance to change, before you want to commit yourself to it. But once we have overcome our resistance and reluctance to change, there may be a willingness to experiment with what we think is the 'ideal self.' So if you really want to change, be more spiritual, or what ever your goal is, try to have a clear vision. And, **Start by starting**. (Meryl Steep)

Top Tips

- Don't set goals that are too large, so that they seem impossible to achieve. **Unrealistic expectations make change a non-starter.**
- If the goal is too demanding, soften it, and if it is too modest, harden it.
- Break your goal into small achievable nuggets set over a realistic timeframe.
- Work out what you need to make it happen including addressing potential pitfalls, so that you always have a provision for a back up or plan B.
- At every stage, review your progress and change things that aren't working.
- You will need an incentive, so keep reminding yourself why change is so important to you, and ask,' What happens if I don't do it?'
- Know you are now just preparing yourself for a new adventure, a new meaningful life.

- Begin looking forward to the future with trust and anticipation—being open and receptive to the process of change.
- Know that you are safe; trust yourself, the Supreme Being (If you believe in God) and the process of change.
- Know that it's fine to let go of the past, and to look forward to a new spiritual life—a life with a purpose and meaning.
- **It is not the strongest of the species that survives, or the most intelligent, but the one most responsive to change.** (Charles Darwin). Such species have an ecological niche to exist.
- **Change will only survive if we live it, nourish it and love it.**

The difficulty arises when we do not go on an inward journey to search for life's purpose, and are not ready for change, but believe that acquisition of material wealth, power and being respected can lead to a happy meaningful life. But can they fill the emptiness of our lives?

Respect—Why do you Need it?

We all want others to respect us, but we hardly ever have any high regard for others. In fact in England in 2008, a young man stabbed another youth because he was not 'shown due respect'. Parents want respect from their offspring. People in authority or high positions want those below them on the hierarchical ladder to defer to their wishes. Gang leaders want gang members to treat them like demigods. Being 'respected' in the broader society is different from being respected in a sub-culture.

In the subculture of hip hop and street culture, 'diss' means to insult—or more often to fail to show sufficient fear in the face of intimidation.

When gang leaders say that they want to feel respected what they are looking for is to be feared, because when people are scared of them they can get away with anything.

Why do we want to be respected? When somebody shows respect to us, it fills a great need, we feel we are somebody, our dignity is maintained and our **ego is boosted**. Why can't we have mutual respect? The human spirit is there in all of us, there is no body low or high. If we believe in the humanity of humankind, then we shall not be respecting the social status or material possessions of others, but their character, dignity and humanness. There will be a genuine recognition of self and others, and respect will be automatic rather than forced.

One of the universal principles of practically all the mainstream religions and philosophies is that, 'we can experience a sense of release if we do not cling to our selfhood but are prepared to give it up. Selfishness, greed and self-preoccupation are perhaps, engrained in our thoughts and behaviour, but are also the source of so much of our pain. Once you gave up strong craving to promote yourself, denigrate others, draw attention to your unique and special qualities and ensure that you were the first in the pecking order, you experienced an immense relief.'

We seek respect from others because of our inflated egos or ego chasing. It is the 'I'—that very core of our being that defines us as a particular person. The 'I' is vulnerable to aversion and hatred. It is attracted to what ever pleases the 'self' and has aversion to what ever threatens this 'I'. So if Joe Bloggs is shown respect by Jane, Joe Blogs will be pleased, but if Jane denigrates Joe Boggs, then, he will not be a very happy man, and may wish to destroy Jane's happiness or even harm her.

When I do not value myself I need others to value me. We go along with others, do what others are doing because we want to be accepted, to be respected by them. It is because a lack of inner strength. Inner strength has to be developed, and once developed, like wisdom; no body can take it from you. Scarcity of self value cannot be remedied by money, recognition, affection attention or influence. Self worth is self compassion, not self pity; it is realising the potential for spiritual growth your struggles offer you. It is the awareness that you are worthy of your life, recognising that that you are part of the community of humanity, with a responsibility to have a meaningful life.

We look at one or two actions of a person's behaviour and condemn the person instead of the perceived wrong acts. We entertain the belief that 'I am good, and others are not as good or wise as I am'. But the reality is that we are not as virtuous as we think we are and others are not bad as we might imagine. It is a perception and perceptions should not be treated as reality.

You can love others only if you love yourself. If you have low self esteem, self hatred or lack self respect, then you can hardly be in a position to love and respect others. Self contempt, or self loathing is a mental state that is directed at yourself, and it might be in opposition to hold others in high regard. Genuine respect for others has to be heartfelt, if it is forced, it can easily turn into revulsion and hatred.

Since we are part of the same Soul, or made 'In his Image,' we merit each other's respect. It should not be reserved for the strong, the powerful and the wealthy people only. Every one has a duty of service to their fellow human beings irrespective of nation, class / caste, race or creed. This will create among all human beings a rational cosmos, a better Community and an ideal individual within it.

If you are feeling sorry for yourself, you are bound to hold others responsible for your woes. It is not a positive state of mind, it is an excessive feeling that things aren't going well for you. Normally when such feelings prevail, we hold others responsible. Instead of seeking respect from others, we can reverse the trend. We need to become more respectful to the needs of our emotional brain for harmony and peacefulness.

Identity Linked to Material Wealth

What do you get a man who has everything?

May I suggest a gravestone inscribed with the words, 'So what?'

(Comedian –Simon Manners)

We have some snobs and status- conscious people in this world who judge the worth of others not by what they are inside, but by their position or wealth. Snobbery is unattractive precisely because snobs do not give people the attention they deserve because of something of no great importance. A rich person cannot be said to be better than a poor person, and a person who bears an inherited tile or is the offspring of a highly placed official has no claim to being any better than you or me. As the old saying has it, we should not pay attention to the bed in which a person is born.

Wealth is valuable in many different ways, in that one can meet one's commitments and pay off one's debts. Wealth contributes greatly to one's ability to avoid unintentional cheating or lying, though it must be said some very rich people have been known to cheat others for paltry sums of money. The wealthy can also consider which charity to support, how to help the needy, where as a poor person may not be able to afford the luxury.

The trappings of affluence—a large house, jewellery, top of the range car etc. have a negative effect on our mental health because they set people up in opposition to one another. This causes what has been called 'status anxiety,' and people with 'status' do not want to lose it.

The really wealthy would be concerned about the Inland Revenue, burglars and kidnappers. There is a worry about losing money that can be as preoccupying as worrying about not having any. Look into the eyes of the mega- rich, those who are included in the Rich List of a country. Carefree? I doubt it. Some may envy Mr. Richman's car, but Joe Blogg will be worried about losing it, or it being damaged or vandalized. Recently an owner of a well known luxury car in England was involved in a serious accident and the driver of the other car was killed. It was reported in the court by the police that the owner of the luxury car was concerned about the damage to his vehicle only. Judging our success or failure in life on our accumulation of objects generates fear of losing them and hence unhappiness. A colleague of mine bought a small budget car, because research showed that car thieves were unlikely to target the said brand.

Those who specifically use power, status or wealth as ways of defining themselves are at particular risk because they are the ones who have the most to lose during economic downturns. The mighty fall, and we should always remember the temporality of earthly things. The **Wheel of Fortune**, or *Rota Fortunae*, is a concept in medieval and ancient philosophy referring to the capricious nature of fate. The Roman philosopher Boethius wrote in *Consolation of Philosophy*:

'I know how Fortune is ever most friendly and alluring to those whom she strives to deceive, until she overwhelms them with grief beyond bearing when least expected....Ah! dull witted mortal, if Fortune begins to stay still, she is no longer Fortune.'

Quite a few rich people commit suicide when their business has failed and they can't maintain their usual standard of living. Having vast amounts of wealth, and then losing it, can have devastating effects if your identity or status is based on the wealth only. This happens because we worship the false gods of material things, and kneel in obeisance at the altar of wealth.

Sometimes economies take a down turn as it is happened in 2008, and because of the recession, people lose their jobs, affluent people lose millions, middle class people lose their status, businesses go into liquidation, and what we had sacrificed our working lives for, turn out to be false idols, and we think that it is the end of the world.

Material advancement sometimes solves one problem, but creates another. One big advantage of acquiring wealth is that it relieves the lower needs in the hierarchy, which then focuses us on the higher needs which we had ignored whilst we sought to raise ourselves high enough so as not to have to worry about the base needs again. But certain people acquire wealth, a good education and high social standing, yet if you observe them, they are not happy. Talk to them, and if they are frank, they will admit that they acquire temporary happiness through external pleasures and experiences, but *real* happiness eludes them. They take sleeping pills and drink excessively. Something is missing, something still not satisfied, so these people take refuge in drugs or in a bottle. Material wealth alone does not resolve the problem of humanity's suffering.

Competitive desire is a social instinct. If you see your neighbour with a new gizmo, you probably want it. Had you never known that they had it, you would have not missed it. But once you have seen it, it might open a huge desire in your life. Most of us, when we are thinking clearly though, want nothing to do with a thing like the new gizmo, but the spirit is weak.

It is possible that this can be seen as a blinkered view of human behaviour or a sad commentary, but some of us do watch what our neighbours or close relatives and friends have. It may be a flashy car, or the most fashionable dress, but if you have it, then I want it as well. I suppose that is why one of the Commandments is, 'Not to be covetous.' Covetousness could be towards some body's cow or car, wife or partner. The Ten Commandments though originally addressed to adult male Israelites, are generally understood to be the moral law of the universal kind and not to be seen as applicable to one community only.

In the frenzy of modern life we lose sight of the real meaning, and the right purpose of our life. People become the sum total of what they produce. Human beings act like machines whose function is to make money. Humans are not for money, money is for humans.

Money should not be our master. We need enough to live of course, as basic necessities like food, clothes, a flat or a house are not free. So money is necessary, but we also need to realize that too much attachment to wealth does not help at all. Ambition is normal. If we seek to do only what our forefathers did, learn only what they learnt, society will not move forward. But ambition also cannot be given free rein, sometimes it needs to be kept under control.

All the saints of the world tell us, the wealthier one becomes, the more suffering one endures. This happens because the person becomes over fond of wealth, because it is something that they are good at creating. **Earning a thousand, man runs after a *lakh*.** (One hundred thousand) **He is never satisfied in his pursuit wealth**. (Guru Granth Sahib)

There is nothing wrong with improving your life situation, but you need to ask yourself—at what cost? Are you stressed? Are you so busy getting to the future that the present is reduced to a means of getting there? The fact that every one else is doing it doesn't mean you have to follow them like sheep. May be it's time to sit back and consider deeply about your life and its suffering. Our quest for material success can also make us blind to the suffering of others. People pursue their self- centred ends, and never challenge their selfish and individualistic culture. There is no time to think or to focus on helping others. There is no time to for the family, the community or the society.

As a matter fact a study tells us that wanting to outdo the neighbours or keeping up with the Joneses is bad for our health. A better way is to help your neighbours and help yourself to the 'good life.' "Man may well be a social animal but constantly looking over one's shoulder seems to make the world a less happy, more unequal place," according to the authors of the Europe –wide study. The study was done in 2009 by Professor Andrew Clark and Claudia Senik. People who live in a "we-economy"—a system of selfless giving and sharing instead of self-centred, competitive approach—are happier. So may be it's time:

- To look objectively at hollow materialism, to take stock, and lift our hearts to a higher, more spiritual plane.
- Reflect on your heart's desire and search for what you are really looking for in life.

The great Zen master Rinzai would often raise his finger and ask his students, "What at this moment is lacking?" A similar question in the Zen tradition is this: "If not now, when?"

Craving for Power

'I put for a general inclination of all mankind, a perpetual and restless desire for power after power that ceases only in death.' (Leviathan, 1651)

Linked closely to our desire for more and more wealth, is our craving for power. The Oxford dictionary defines *power* as the 'capacity to influence the behaviour of others, the emotions or the course of events. 'Sociologists say that *Power* is the ability of holders to exact compliance or obedience of other individuals to their will, on whatsoever basis. The desire for power in relationships, between societies and nations never ceases. Based on international influence and military strength, we have super powers and world powers.

It is said that when Alexander the Great (356-323 BC) was coming down the Khyber Pass after conquering Persia and Egypt to invade India, he saw a sadhu or an ascetic resting under a tree. The ascetic did not stir when the huge army was passing by but just lay in the shade. Alexander was surprised at the holy man's nonchalance so he sent a soldier to fetch the sadhu. The ascetic refused to move, so Alexander walked up to him.

Alexander was educated by the philosopher Aristotle and was a cultured man. He was curious about the sadhu and wanted to find out how a person could be so detached and not be impressed by the might of his army. The dialogue between them went something like this:

Sadhu: Who are you?

Alexander: I am Alexander of Macedonia.

Sadhu: What are you doing in India?

Alexander: I am here to conquer India?

Sadhu: What will you do after conquering India?

Alexander: I shall conquer other countries.

Sadhu: What will you do after you have conquered the whole world?

Alexander: I shall rest after conquering the whole world.

Sadhu: Why can't you rest *now* like me instead of causing suffering and destruction, spreading misery where ever you go, killing innocent people, and watching your soldiers being killed?

Alexander fought one of his fiercest battles against the rajah Porus in the Punjab, and his depleted troops refused to go further and they forced his retreat. Alexander the Great died in Babylon of malarial fever at the age of 33 years. Alexander it seems had no time to rest; his short life was spent in acquisition of power and conquests only. Some of the high fliers of today also get burnt out at a very young age because they also chase wealth, status (respect) and power.

Appreciate What we Have

It is said that a pious noble man was passing through a village when he heard a young man crying. The nobleman stopped his horse and asked the reason for his wailing. The young ma said that he had no money. He had nothing which he could call his own. The nobleman told the young man that if he looked closely at himself, he would realize that he had a lot. The young man indicated that he was miserable at it was, and would appreciate if his condition was not made worse. The nobleman told the young man that he would give him 1,000 gold coins if he would give him both his eyes. The young man thought for a minute, and said that he doesn't want to be blind. The nobleman offered the same amount for one eye but the young man said that he wouldn't like to lose an eye.

The nobleman then offered 1,000 gold coins for both the hands. but the young man said that he wouldn't be able to survive without his hands. The nobleman then offered him 500 gold coins for one hand, but again the young man refused to lose his hand. The nobleman then turned his attention to the feet and offered him 1000 coins for both the feet followed by 500 gold coins for one foot. Both the offers were spurned without a second's thought.

The moral of the story is that he had a lot to be thankful for but did not recognise his real assets. His mind was focused on material possessions. This is not to say that money is not important, but then money is not everything also. 'Money will buy you a pretty good dog but it won't buy the wag of his tail.' We need to look at what we have and be thankful. Once we recognise that we probably have what really matters to us most, like our health, (which is singularly important) our values, our well being, we can work out strategically as to how we can acquire other things for our subsistence also. If you have a good dog, you can always work out how to get the wag of its tail.

Time for Reflection

When times are hard, like, or gloomy because of recession or depression, perhaps, can prove to be a good opportunity for people (unwelcome for some) to take stock of their lives and pause for reflection. Some religious leaders reported during the economic downturn in 2009 that they get a sense that tectonic plates are shifting. The national mood was changing, that people after many years of unbridled consumerism were turning their backs upon hollow materialism and lifting their hearts to a higher, more spiritual plane.

People working in the commercial and financial institutions looked back on their professional, personal and academic experience to gain a deeper understanding of their personal development, and real job satisfaction from what they were doing. After much searching for the truth about themselves and their life they decided to change. They wanted do something worth while in their lives and some embarked on training as teachers or social workers. They took on jobs which were less paying but more rewarding and more fulfilling. To survive on less income, they embraced the old values of frugality and caring for others. You don't need a degree in divinity to understand that over consumerism, materialism and self indulgence are morally wrong and we have a duty to others also who are perhaps less unfortunate. Besides personal responsibility, we also have social responsibility.

Self- knowledge, which is what makes your heart really happy, will help you to realize what is really important to you and gives meaning to your life. An open heart allows one to feel from inside, what it is all about. This is a kind of knowing that is different to that of the intellect; it is more visceral and direct. It is a deep connection with oneself, which expresses itself when you stop worrying about being what the others say, being self conscious and just bow to the spirit inside you. When I do it with an open heart, it reminds me of what is important to me, of my values, and becomes a focus through which I can reorient myself

Spriritua lity

Religion is not identical with spirituality; rather religion is the form spirituality takes in civilisation.

(William Irwin Thompson)

Spirituality according to most adherents is an essential part of an individual's health and well-being. It makes their life more meaningful.

However, people have different key concepts when asked what spirituality means to them. Some think that spirituality is closely linked to their particular faith and others do not want to bring in religion at all. What they want to understand is 'me', the sense of self, relationships and life priorities. According to them a belief in God is an article of faith, not consistent with scientific understandings of the world. Hard-line rationalists argue that religions are ludicrous sets of beliefs spread by the gullible. Rationalism has a belief in reason rather than religion as a guiding principle in life. The problem with rationalism is that such a belief must by its very nature deny anything which it perceives as metaphysical.

However, 'the rationalism of ancient Greece was not opposed to religion; indeed, it was itself a faith tradition that evolved its own distinctive version of the principles that guided most of the religious traditions.' According to Karen Armstrong, *philosophia*[3] was a yearning for a transcendent wisdom; it had a healthy respect for the *logos*[4], and held that the highest wisdom was rooted in unknowing and its insights were the result of practical meditative exercises and a disciplined lifestyle.

In the current world, science has become a substitute for religion in many cases. People with a scientific bent try to use it as a block when one tries to tell them about one's faith. Karen Armstrong says that scientific rationalism consists largely of problem-solving, an approach that does lead to systematic advance: after a problem has been solved, it can be laid aside and scientists can move onto tackle the next. But the humanities do not function in this way, because the problem they confront, such as mortality, grief, evil or the nature of happiness, are not capable of a once-and-for-all time solution.

When we are happy, and everything is fine in our life, we do not want to think of anything else except how to enjoy life. But when things are not going that smoothly, it could be the break up of the family, financial crises, passing away of some one close to us or when an individual faces the thought of one's own death. Then we start looking for some thing deeper, our moorings and our inner strength. You examine your values and priorities and may be embrace new ones. Spiritual practice is not about externals, how you look etc. Spiritual practice takes place in our hearts and minds. True change is within. It is your attitude to life that truly reflects an improved mind and heart.

For example, unlike many mind altering drug related experiences, the experiences related by transformed people, or people who had embraced spirituality because some experiences, conveyed a sense of the sacred and a sense of responsibility towards others and the world about them. Two fifth of the subjects according to William R. Miller author of *Quantum Change—When Epiphanies and Sudden Insights Transform Ordinary Lives* did not believe in God, but they became more spiritual, less materialistic and more compassionate towards others and themselves. There was a uniform decrease in the value placed on 'wealth', 'attractiveness', 'popularity', and 'fitting' in, and an increase in 'spirituality,' 'personal peace' 'forgiveness' and 'loving'. What was changed was 'me', the sense of self.

Some questions which may help you to be clearer about Spirituality:

1. What is it about Spirituality that intrigues you?
2. What is it that makes you want to lead a more spiritual life?

Research by Martsolf and Mickley (1998) highlighted the following areas as worth considering when understanding spirituality:

- **Meaning**-significance of life, making sense of situations, deriving a purpose.
- **Values**-beliefs, standards and ethics that are cherished.
- **Transcendence**- the state of being beyond the reach or apprehension of experience. (Opposite is immanence). The *New Fontana Dictionary of Modern Thought* definition is:

awareness and appreciation of 'a transcendent dimension to life' to life beyond, self.

- **Connecting**- increased awareness of a connection between self and others- God / Spirit/Divine and Nature.
- **Becoming**-an unfolding of life that demands reflection and experience, includes who one is and how one knows.

One aspect of 'Being spiritual' is goal directed with aims such as simultaneously to improve one's wisdom, lessen attachment to material wealth and false ideas. It can only be done if we take responsibility for our own spiritual lives, to help ourselves to seek knowledge.

Those of you who have a faith will most probably say that my Religion has been set out to answer the above questions. As regards the medical or health aspect, an American doctor, Daniel Hall of the University of Pittsburgh, has sought to tackle the matter of benefits of religious belief in a scientifically robust way by assessing how several different medical treatments measure up when compared to the well documented benefits of religious belief in increasing life expectancy by some three years. Dr. Hall concludes: "The practical significance of regular religious attendance is similar to several widely recommended therapies and may well be more cost effective."

For people who have a faith, the central defining characteristic of spirituality is a sense of connection to a 'whole' which includes emotional experience of awe and reverence. It is a connection with God, the Supreme Being, Divine or what ever you call it through their religion. For the believers, religion has given shape and meaning to most lives. They find spiritual development and inner peace through prayer, reading and reflecting on the scriptures and meditation. Research published by Professor Bruce Hood at Bristol University in September 2006 suggests that belief in religions runs deep and it will continue as we are hard wired to believe in God. However, some would argue that we are not hardwired to believe in God, but we have an inherent belief in something greater than ourselves. They may perceive this as something other than 'God.'

Religions have a lot to teach us, and most of us respect the scriptures and the great works by Prophets, Messengers and Gurus, but the real treasure is rarely tapped. By merely reading or listening with no application is not of much benefit. Science in the laboratory is of little use unless taken advantage of or converted to technology for our use in our house. So start with self reflection and try to incorporate the teachings of the sages in your life. But let no one dictate to you regarding what you should do and not do in your spiritual life. Let the ultimate authority be the authority of your spirit within you, not that of any man or woman. The ultimate reality can be found only because:

Man you are made of Divine essence;

Recognise thyself

(Guru Granth Sahib)

Light

There is an interesting story from the Buddhist tradition about king Bibimsala of Magadha who had decided to honour a visit by Gautama Buddha with a Festival of Light. The houses were freshly painted and massive garlands of flowers were hung across the street. The greatest display of all was made by the thousands of brass lamps that lined the main street, creating a fantastic tunnel of lights for the Buddha to walk through.

There was an old lady living within the city who although very poor, was rich for the love of Gautama Buddha. She only had an old cracked, clay oil lamp for which she made a wick out of a torn sari, but she had no money for fuel. A kindly shopkeeper, taking pity on her, offered a little bit of oil to keep her lamp alight for sometime. She excitedly took her place at the edge of the street looking expectantly towards the gates for the Buddha to appear.

As dusk began to settle, Gautama Buddha emerged followed by a train of disciples, their bare feet padding silently on the soft sand. The king's face was a picture of pride as he surveyed the magnificent display of glittering lamps lining the pathway. But his look of pleasure soon turned to horror as a huge gust of wind blew through the gates, extinguishing every lamp except one—a cracked old clay lamp, carefully shielded against the wind by an old lady. Gautama Buddha stopped in front of her. As she knelt down to receive his blessing he said to his disciples, 'observe this woman carefully. Nothing can extinguish the woman's light because of the power and strength of her devotion. As long as spiritual disciplines are practised with the kind of love and dedication as this woman has, the 'Light' will never go out.'

A Spritual Life

Raise yourself to such an extent that before chalking out the destiny, the Supreme Being asks a person what their desire is.

(Translation of a couplet from an Urdu poem by Allma Iqbal)

In daily life a really spiritual person would be displaying some or all of the 12 qualities and characteristics:

1. Would be pure without any stains on their personal self. Tries to control evil desires at all times.
2. Would earn his living by honest means, but not be attached to or overly fond of worldly possessions. Such a person remains non-attached just like a lotus remains detached from the mud in the water.
3. Looks upon all alike and does not differentiate on the basis of colour, creed or gender. Sees all creation as one.
4. Has great patience to bear every eventuality. Takes both comforts and grief in their stride.
5. Has the quality of filling vacuums around them with fragrance.

6. Displays virtues where he /she may be.

7. Has no egoistical pride in their mind, always endeavours to live in humility. Does not consider himself superior to others.

8. Honour and dishonour: A spiritual person retains the equanimity and does not let honour or dishonour disturb it. When the whole world is praising / flattering you, you do not let that get that into your head. And, when people are condemning you or finding faults in you, you do not feel down hearted and abandon the good work you are doing. The work ought to be for the common good and not for self aggrandisement. You will persist unwaveringly, in the full appreciation that glory and grace or condemnation and put downs are transient and not fixed.

9. Treats every one like their friend, and does not cultivate evil thoughts or enmity towards anyone.

10. Is always impartial.

11. Seeks spiritual wisdom to enlighten her mind, and lives a meaningful life.

12. Believes in truth and nothing but the truth.

Daily Practice

- If possible, try to help others. If that is not possible, at least do no harm to other. This can be done by developing a strong desire to refrain from harming others physically or emotionally.

- Plant trees of friendship at every step. If you have planted a seedling of enmity, uproot the young plant before it grows into a full tree. It will only have thorns and pain that will hurt you as well.

- When we consider that we have enemies, our mind can never be at rest. 'No one is my enemy, and no one is a stranger to me. I have befriended the whole world.' (Guru Granth Sahib).

Let us live joyfully

Let us form a community of love, in a world full of hatred.

Let us live without any kind of hatred.

Let us live joyfully,

Let us form a community of spiritual health, in a world full of illness,

Let us live without any kind of disease.

Let us live joyfully,

Let us form a community of peace, in a world full of rivalry,

Let us live without any kind of rivalry.

—Let us live on spiritual bliss, radiating spiritual light.

(From the Dhammapada (500BCE-2000CE) India)

Lessons from Nature

Modern world has gathered its wealth and missed its well-being. (Rabindranath Tagore)

Rabindranath Tagore was awarded the Nobel Prize for Literature in 1913.He has been acclaimed as perhaps the greatest literary figure in history. He has written innumerable poems, songs plays, novels and essays covering every important social, political, and cultural issue of his time. Tagore believed that nature is created both as man's home and also as an instrument which, through its beauty awakens the human heart and directs it towards the Supreme Being. Just as an artist creates a work of art both to express and evoke a certain mood, the Supreme Being creates the world of nature to evoke love in the human being. We live in an increasingly urbanized world and are not in touch with the realities of the natural world.

Rabindranath Tagore was taking a walk early one the morning with his friends when suddenly he started dancing with joy near a mound of rubbish. The municipality of the town used to collect all the rubbish and pile it up in one place to dispose of it later. On being asked the reason for his dancing, Rabindranath Tagore said that he had just observed another beauty of nature. Sun's rays do not distinguish between a clean and dirty place. They fall equally every where.

The sun gives the warmth to every one. The air equally touches the king and the poor.

Connecting with the Supreme Being

As I prepare to go about my work today,

may my intention to live in your present moment

be the pattern for this day and my life.

With your help, may I forever do

Only one thing at a time—

Always I communion with you, my Beloved

With all my heart and mind and soul.

(Modern prayer by Edward Hays, USA)

We have already discussed a search for meaning in life, and values can lay the foundation of morality which in turn can lead to spirituality. Some people do not believe in a God who transcends our normal or physical experience, and is not subject to the limitations of the material universe, but those who do believe in a Supreme Being do yearn for a connection.

It was during the process of revelation and the vision of God, that Guru Nanak recited the *mul mantra*, the basis concept. According to Sangat Singh in *Sikhs in History*, 'this constitutes the core of Sikh philosophy and provides the quintessence of the teachings of the Gurus and Bhaktas (Devotees) contained in Guru

Granth Sahib. It is paraphrased by Professor Jodh Singh with whom some well known scholars agree as:

This Being is One. He is eternal. He is the creator of all things. He is immanent in his creation. He is without fear and without enmity. This Being is not subject to time. He is beyond birth and death. He is himself responsible for his own manifestation. (He is known) by the Guru's grace.

Eckhart Tolle makes a relevant point when he says in, *The Power of Now*, that the word God has become empty of meaning through thousands of years of misuse. He explains it thus: "By misuse, I mean that people who have never even glimpsed the realm of the sacred, the infinite vastness behind that word, use it with great conviction, as if they knew what they were talking about. Or they argue against it, as if they knew what they were denying. This mistake gives rise to absurd beliefs, assertions, and egoistic delusions, such as 'my or our God as the only true God, and your God is false,' or Nietzsche's famous statement—God is dead."

Even people who should know better, the so called 'religious people' also fall into the same trap and normally say my God is called this or that and my God is different from your God. They make God who is boundless and omnipresent into a finite and tribal / parochial entity. Guru Gobind Singh, the tenth Guru of the Sikhs says: "God is not called by any particular name. He does not exist at any particular place, and he has no caste, no outline, colour or mark. He elaborates this when he says: "God has no particular country no dress, no outline, and no love for any particular thing. "God is present at every place, on every side and in every colour. His universal love exists every where. His Light is visible. He is present every where."

Karen Armstrong very aptly describes **Being** as: The fundamental energy that supports, animates, and sustains everything that exists; to be carefully distinguished from *a being*, which is finite, particular and limited manifestation of Being itself.

It is not the remit of this book to talk about the existence of the Supreme Being, but I feel that I must mention here the experience of a top level scientist who had a malignant tumour. I have heard and read about miracles, but never paid much heed to them because of lack of evidence. Anyway, I have seen Vasunder Bharadwaj on television three or four times addressing audiences and every time he had a file of notes and letters from doctors and surgeons with him. He had treatment in the States where he worked as a scientist but to no avail. He came to India but again his condition did not improve. Then his wife suggested that he prays at the Golden Temple, Amritsar in Punjab. Bharadwaj's personal testimony is that he went to Amritsar in an ambulance as he was in the throes of death. As Sukhmanee (the Psalm of peace) from Guru Granth Sahib was being recited, he was reclining on his bed, but suddenly he felt some vibrations—Bharadwaj calls them 'waves of energy' and he got up and sat down. His daughter luckily had a camera, and sensing that something extraordinary was happening, recorded the whole episode. As he had tumour in his brain, he had been deaf for a long time, but suddenly found that he could hear. As he carried on listening to the recitation, he could feel his body gaining in strength, and he listened to the remaining readings.

After the recovery, he went to see his doctors who could not believe their eyes and after various tests, pronounced that his tumour was no longer malignant but had become benign. He was out of danger. A speaker who introduced him to audiences and congregations called it a miracle, but he says that it is not a miracle, it is God's will, and the Supreme Being wanted him to **live for a purpose.** Some people say that science and religion are incompatible, but it must be said that the Vatican employs scientists (usually monks with formal scientific training) to look into claims of miracles.

If we acknowledge that, God is the Primal, a separate Being, who is also the Creator of the Universe, and the soul of the individual is a part, a spark of the Primal Soul, then we can believe that 'we are all one family. God is One, yet He can be seen in innumerable forms created by Him. "God is the Primal Soul. All souls originate from God's Soul" Guru Gobind Singh explains this when he says: "He is present in all. (At the same time) He is separate from all. God has only one Form, without any parallel. God himself manifests as a poor man, a lord, or a king at different places."

It is believed that Kabir (d1518) who has his own following in India, said that 'Allah and Rama are but different names for the same Godhead." Some believe that Kabir was the son of a high caste Brahmin who was brought up by a Muslim weaver. Kabir says, 'God is called by many names: Hari (Krishna) and Ram in Hinduism, Allah, Karim and Rahim (the Merciful One) in Islam. What is important is finding God beyond the names, and not to limit the Supreme Being. "Hari dwells in the east (Banaras—Home of Krishna) they say, and Allah resides in the west (Mecca—centre of Muslim pilgrimage): **search** for him in the heart of your heart, for that is where he dwells, Rahim, Ram. All men and women ever born are nothing but forms of God."

Introspection

What we are today comes from our thoughts of yesterday. And our present thoughts build our life of tomorrow; our life is a creation of our mind.

Epicurus says that if there is a deity, it is a blessed and tranquil being. We can treat the idea of such a deity as a model for us to emulate, its peacefulness, and detachment are exactly what we should seek to achieve in our lives.

We grow to be like the things we contemplate, meditation on God will make us godlike. Guru Nanak in the mul mantra says that God has no **enmity** and is without **fear**. Whether you have a religion is irrelevant here, we all need these virtues. We have to ask our selves some painful questions: Do I have enemies? How many? Enmity also leads to hatred, which can engulf you more than the subject of your ire. Ask yourself: 'Is it **a fact** that the other person is bad or is it your perception?' Each one of us is a summation of our habits and experiences, so it is inevitable that we see things in our own way. We live in our own unique and separate individual worlds. Our perceptions are coloured by our upbringing and conditioning.

Imagine that you are like a house. It has an outside which most people see and form an opinion about you, but few people explore indoors. Even we ourselves don't bother to go beyond our exterior, to explore the richness and diversity of both the pleasant and the unpleasant aspects of our inner make up.

When challenges come, as they always do in our lives, make it a habit to go within. When you focus within and feel the inner body, you immediately become still and present as you are not following the dictates of your mind. Once you are in the present, you will not be run by your mind and following your disposition to act in certain ways. For example, you will not be resorting to physical or psychological violence, 'to teach' your perceived enemy a lesson. You might like to assume that, things can be changed. Enmity can be changed into friendship, hatred into love, that nothing is set in stone and everything is negotiable. Go with an 'open hand rather than with a clenched fist' like Barrack Obama, the president of the United States says. Figure out what your aspirations are, but have some sense of the beliefs and aspirations of the other party as well. Go for a win—win outcome and see love triumphing over hatred and the enemy becoming a friend. We are supposed to be intelligent beings, higher beings, so we must act according to our higher selves. Growing wisdom leads to a more meaningful and fulfilling life.

Some people question as to why we have so much hate and suffering in this world if the Supreme Being is benign. There have been natural disasters which have caused havoc and devastation. But if we look at world history, most great tragedies that involved terrible loss of life and property were brought about by human beings. We humans make the mess. Today all over the world people live in constant fear of racial, ethnic, religious and economic conflict. Who is responsible for this fear? Not animals. Sometimes we blame religions for causing conflicts and terrorism. It's not religion which causes the rifts but extreme ideologies which encourage some young people to embrace extreme measures. The main concern of the religions is betterment of humanity, to make our lives as meaningful as possible, and not to destroy others. Ideologies in the current climate can be seen as justifications which mask some set of interests, or a belief system which can be used to mobilize people for actions.

Ideas no doubt do not wield swords, drop bombs or launch missiles. It is not ideas in themselves that cause wars, it is people and their interpretation of ideas who cause wars. According to Karen Armstrong, 'Religion is a practical discipline that teaches us to discover new capacities of mind and heart. Some people will be better at it than others, some people appallingly inept, and others will miss the point entirely.' Some people get their religion right, and try to uplift themselves spiritually, and others take advantage of it to further their own ends. Religion is different from religious people.

Contemporary fundamentalism in different religions is an essentially modern phenomenon, and unlike its medieval counterparts, it has been less engaged in Theology or Philosophy and more concerned with ideology and politics. Fundamentalists are committed to political and social change. Their ideology can be checked and counteracted by the right knowledge about the essence of the scriptures, a lot of the certainty which the ideologues hold can be undermined. Let us see what a Persian Sufi Muslim has to say about religions:

With one Voice

In the adoration and the benedictions of the righteous

The praises of all the prophets are kneaded together.

All their praises are mingled into one stream,

All the vessels are emptied into one ewer,

Because He that is praised is, in fact, only One.

In this respect all religions are only one religion,

Because all praises are directed toward God's light

(Jalil al–Din Rumi)

Fighting Injustice

"Nothing is easier than to denounce the evil doer. Nothing is more difficult than to understand him. (Dostoevsky) If evil is intended, then you have to resist it, and not accept it. You have to find out how to fight the injustice in spite of the fear. You are in control of your life with your principles and values, live according to those, and you are a rebel to the tyranny of some one who chooses it as a way of life. You may wish to make a resolution like the following:

I will be truthful,

I will suffer no injustice,

I will be free from **fear,**

I will not use force,

I will be of good to all men.

(Mahatma Gandhi)

Gandhi says that he will not use force to fight injustice or tyranny. Gandhi made the concept of ahimsa—which stands for respect for all living things and avoidance of violence towards others, popular.

If you do not want to live in fear then try to live according to the Golden Rule, do not frighten others.

One, who does not terrify others and is not afraid of others;

Should be held as the *Gianni* (True Saint) possessing Divine Knowledge, hear O mind (maṇ) says Nanak.

(Guru Granth Sahib)

Facing Fear

Fear and anger are two strong and powerful emotions in our repertoire. Real fear says Robert Winston in *The Human Mind and How to Make the Most of It,* results in massive changes in the body's systems which control blood flow and indeed people can drop dead from fear alone if the heart ceases its normal pulsation. The unique power of fear makes sense in evolutionary terms. Our ancestors were never safe from predators and other perils. Even now, if you are walking at night in a tropical country and you see something in your path, whether it is a snake or just a piece of rope when focus your torch on it can assist your survival.

Fear can be a unique underlying motivator or destroyer in our lives. Fear can turn people into victims, causing them to feel overwhelmed, weak and hopeless. Most of us are afraid of hate, rejection, life, death and—the unknown. When we are concerned with these fears, we are focusing outside ourselves. Instead of feeding the fears, we will be better off refocusing on the purpose and meaning in life. Being attentive to the present moment will shift your focus.

According to Edmund Burke, "No passion so effectively robs the mind of all its powers of acting and reasoning as fear." Franklin Roosevelt said that, "We have nothing to fear but fear itself." Quite often the fear has no basis, but at times it can be genuine too. So at some times we have to acknowledge the fear and see what can be done with it. If it is fear from the past, which has become fixed in your mind, it is definitely beneficial to discuss it and get it out.

The person you have feared might not have intended to instil fear in you. I once had a practice teacher who would look at me with partly closed eyes, completely focused on me. I thought that he was not happy with my performance, and I asked him one day as to why he always looked at me so sternly. The truth was that he had a squint in one eye, and had to look at me with partly closed eyes, so that the gaze of the problem eye did not deviate.

Wallowing in fear accomplishes nothing. If you open up to the feeling, and are comfortable expressing it and acknowledge the fear, or any other feeling, you can overcome the obstacle in your journey toward success. If you hide or deny your feelings, they will stay with you forever. Once you have acknowledged the fear, it's important to get the feelings into perspective. Think of the damaging effect of letting them dominate you. You may decide that the reality is that the feeling has no basis. You can retain the memory of the feelings for sometime to learn the lessons. Once you have reduced their importance to the minimum, or to almost zero, they cannot dominate you. It's only by experiencing them that you can let them go and it's only by letting them go that you can be truly free. When you move forward and through fear, you overcome it. What you resist, you may intensify, exaggerate and become a victim, whether it is anger or fear.

Each time you give into fear, you feel less good about yourself, and a piece of your confidence is eroded—especially when what ever you are doing is the 'right thing' where the judgement was formed by conscience. Each time you overcome a fear you feel a little more brave, a better person.

If you look at the lives of great men and women, their quiet inner knowing, their self confidence and the conviction that what they were doing was the right thing in the circumstances sustained them when the things were not going well.

Enmity

So long as our relationship is defined by our differences, we will empower those who sow hatred rather than peace, and who promote conflict rather than cooperation that can help all our people achieve justice and prosperity. This cycle of suspicion and discord must end.

(President Barack Obama calling for an end to 'cycle of suspicion and discord'—Cairo University, June 2009

In sports we say that we learn from our opponents, they can be your best teacher. Treat them as 'friends,' because you learn how they perform, and then improve and better you own techniques. Don't treat them as your enemy, because when you treat somebody like an enemy, you are consumed with hatred. With an enemy, you can't build your inner strength. Your focus is on the other person and not your own spiritual advancement. During a competition, there can be some bitter rivalries, but the important point is to keep such feelings within the confines of the match and forget them afterwards. Carrying them into your life is not conducive to sportsmanship and can be damaging.

Listen to what you are saying to yourself or your self talk. We are always talking to ourselves; it is what you and 'normal' people do, though we don't do it aloud. The 'self talk' may be reviving the distant past, and the negative outcomes. The self talk may not be relevant to the situation at hand, but it will interpret it in terms of the past. This is because the self talk belongs to your conditioned mind, which is the result of all your past experiences as well as collective cultural influences. So you see and judge the present through the eyes of the past and get a totally distorted view of it. Often the 'self- talk' is a person's worst enemy.

You can free yourself from the 'self–talk' or still your mind by listening to it. This is true liberation. Listen to the self-talk and identify the repetitive thought patterns, the ones which are recurring again and again, Like gramophone old records, they have been playing in your head for many years. Listen to them impartially and try to change them to positive ones. Don't depend on it, or act on it. Remember that the mind has its own mind, and it is not within our control.

The term ego means different things to different people, but I use it to mean what gives you self importance. That is why we are on an ego trip most of the time, we want to feel and increase our sense of self importance. To the ego, past and present are important. It is always concerned with keeping the past alive, because without it a sense of self is no longer there. It constantly projects into the future to ensure its survival, the false sense of self. It is always seeking something new. It is not living in the present. So change your self talk to a more POSITIVE ONE. If the voice is saying: 'I can't bear him or her because of this reason or that reason,' look at all the positive qualities of the person and say, 'I can talk to him. He or she is a human being like me.' Perhaps we both have made mistakes. Be in the present moment rather than being a victim of the past.

One day you may even smile at the antics the mind or the content of your self talk as you would smile at the antics of a child. This means that you are no longer unconsciously identifying with what the mind is saying, as Eckhart Tolle says, 'you no longer take the content of your mind all that seriously, as your sense of self does not depend on it.' You become a 'conscious thinker.' You begin to realize that there is a vast realm of intelligence beyond 'automatic thoughts.' You also realize that all the things that truly matter—making life more meaningful, recognising the purpose of life—arise from beyond the mind. The above can be summed up by saying—'become the master of your mind.'

Once you are free from the dictates of your mind, and the past has lost its hold on you, you can move to the next step—forgiveness. Check if your mind is holding onto a grievance pattern such as blame, resentment or anger that is feeding your enmity. Forgiveness is to relinquish your grievance and so let go of the resentment and grief. It happens naturally once you realist that your enmity or grievance serves no purpose except to give you pain, sleepless nights and 'grief'. Maybe the mind cannot forgive—but you can plant a seed of forgiveness there. You can then get your mind to accept the forgiveness; otherwise the process is not complete. Once you have truly forgiven, you feel like a liberated person with no baggage to carry. You are on your spiritual journey now, because your roots within are becoming deeper.

It is up to you to change the world into a more peaceful and loving place for your children to inherit. Think of the legacy you want to leave. It is your own learning and modelling of forgiveness, understanding, patience and love that teaches your children the same values. You talk about hatred of your enemies, and your children and most probably your grand children will inherit intolerance and hatred towards your enemies. We all have heard of families and communities and nation states where hatred and warfare have been passed on from generation to generation.

An open friendly attitude opens doors in any culture. That is why attractive personalities and 'good mixers' have most success in interpersonal relationships. This does not come from a 'closed fist' but from an open hearted, people- liking- attitude and respect for the views of the others. Indeed your thoughts do create the reality you live in .With positive thoughts and actions, you can create a more positive world. In the end you can honestly say:

No one is my enemy; no one is a stranger to me. I have befriended the whole world.

(Guru Granth Sahib)

Don't Keep the Past Alive

We humans believe that we are the best species in the world, but we can learn from birds how to live and how to die. Observe them closely, and we come to realize that it is only humans who keep grudges and grievances. We make living and dying a problem.

The dove is regarded in Christianity as a symbol of peace, as it is the bird that returned to the Ark with an olive branch. Eckhart Tolle says that ducks have taught him important spiritual lessons. 'How peacefully they float along, at ease with themselves, totally present in the Now, dignified and perfect as only a mindless creature can be. Occasionally, however, two ducks will get into a fight—sometimes for no apparent reason, or because one duck has strayed into another's private space. The fight usually lasts only for a few seconds, and then the ducks separate, swim off in opposite directions, and vigorously flap their wings a few times. They then continue to swim on peacefully as if the fight had never happened. When I observed that for the first time, I suddenly realized that by flapping their wings they were releasing surplus energy, thus preventing it from becoming trapped in their body and turning into negativity. This is natural wisdom, and it is easy for them because they do not have a mind that keeps past alive unnecessarily and then builds an identity around it.'

Footnotes

1. Victor Frankl is a survivor of holocaust, and he developed his psychology and life philosophy as a result of his time in the death camps. At one time he was considered next to Freud and Jung—as the third greatest psychologist.

2. Though 'He ' and 'Him' have been used in the translation, Guru Granth Sahib is gender free.

3. The love of wisdom. (Greek).

4. (Greek): dialogue speech; reasoned logical and scientific thought. Ancient Greek philosophers used the term to denote the pragmatic, accurate mode of thought that was distinct from *mythos.* (Myth.)

Chapter 5

Living a Meaningful Life

It matters not how a man dies, but how he lives. The act of dying is not of importance, it lasts so short a time.

(James Boswell, *Life of Samuel Johnson*)

The question of how to live, the best way to conduct oneself in life, which course of action is right or wrong has been debated since times immemorial. Aristotle believed that, in order to be happy, one has to live a life of virtue, not as a means to an end, but as the realization of that end. 'Virtue does not come by fortune, but by one's efforts. Misfortune can remove it, but virtue is not a capacity that we are born with. Rather we must develop it through practice and the right kind of upbringing.

Those who believe in karma would say that virtue is not a capacity that we are born with. Their view would be that if we live this life virtuously, it would be possible to have it stored in your karma[1] so that when we have our next life, we would have it available.

Education is vital, especially having virtuous people one can emulate. Some people would argue that it is difficult to find virtuous people these days. We can always think of the writers of our scriptures, or philosophical works. Virtue is a habit, but it is a cultivated habit that involves appropriate feeling, and requires experience, that is, practice in choosing. In ethics, Socrates put forward the view that a good person never knowingly does wrong. A good character is established, not by a single good action, but by continual refinement over a lifetime.' "One swallow does not make a summer."

We are born as babies, we flower into youth, and then old age overtakes and then finally comes our departure from this world. Nature takes of that, we can't avoid getting old and some of us die in childhood or when still young. **There is no way to escape death.** We are nourished by mother earth in the sense that we get our food from the earth and a dead body is either cremated or buried. If it is buried, it becomes part of the earth again, in other words our existence is: 'dust to dust.' That is why earth like water (floods etc.—Noah) stands for life as much as for death. A cremated body ends up as ashes which again are either scattered at some *holy* place to mingle with the dust or into a river etc. We have no control over our birth and no body can predict when death will knock at our door.

The Ground On Which I Stand

I am of the nature to grow old:

There is no way to escape growing old…

I am of the nature to die:

There is no way to escape death.

All that is dear to me and everyone I love

Are of the nature to change:

There is no way to escape being separated from them.

My actions are my only true belongings:

I cannot escape the consequences of my actions.

My actions are the ground on which I stand

(Gautama Buddha)

But we can ensure that our actions do not hurt others, but they are for the good of others. Of course, there are times when we cannot ensure this. There are circumstances where we have to choose the lesser of two evils. 'The needs of the many outweigh the needs of the one' to quote the character Spock in Sky Trek. The principles of utilitarianism could be seen as pertinent in such circumstances. The doctrine holds that the happiness of the greatest number should be the guiding principle of conduct.

It is said that self praise is no praise. There is no point in just saying that I will be a virtuous person, and not translating that into action. Guru Nanak says:

'Words do not a sinner or saint make;

Action alone is recorded in the book of fate.

What ever one sows, he reaps...'

Moral code has a high place in practically all the religions. That could be the reason why we have the very terms: High morals, Low morals, No morals. They require their followers to be compassionate, just etc. The teachings of a religion have to be practised—they have to be translated into ethical action. There is not much benefit in reading or reciting them mechanically. Religion is a practical discipline that teaches us to discover new capacities of mind and heart. It will not come because a religion requires it. At the same time we can't magisterially pass judgement on the teachings before embarking on a religious way of life to judge their truth or falsehood. Upholding a moral code, or being truthful or virtuous should arise naturally as a result of one's practice. Buddhism says the Buddha has life force, wisdom and compassion, and that we have the same state of life in us. To seek enlightenment is to reveal this state in our own lives—and in so doing we will gain awareness of our life force, wisdom and compassion.

For Guru Nanak, purity of life is the highest object of human endeavour.

'Truth surpasses all

But higher still is true living.'

Some philosophers, pragmatists and others may argue about the meaning of 'truth,' and put forward the 'argument that truth is relative, 'and we can't assert that 'truth is some sort of absolute.' Again it is something that needs to be practised, that we live to the best of ability, to strain every nerve to live in accordance with the best in us. Truthful living is what we aim for. We can't find the spiritual way by merely talking about it.

To Guru Nanak, inner purity was what counted, not the caste or social status of a person. The heart must be purified of all egoistic and selfish tendencies, so there has to be purity amid impurity, spiritual detachment while shouldering the family responsibility. The Guru explains that just as the lotus flower is not affected by water and always remains much above its surface, however big the rise or fall in its level may be, and just as a water-duck lives in water, swims on it but its wings do not become wet and it can fly away at any time it likes, similarly a mortal has to live in the world, with his or her own family, detached from *maya* (Mammon). Economic security attained through honest labour is the best way for the maintenance of a happy life.

"Work hard and share with others,

Nanak, though shall find the way."

"Regard not that which benefits you but hold to that which benefits mankind," he said, "for what is good for the hive is good for the bee." Greed for possessions, focus on material gains and lack of sharing with others keep you off the true path." In short, your life has a purpose, a meaning, which is to serve others to the best of your ability. That is the driving force which really keeps you alive.

We may have no power over death, but we can ensure that we lead a 'good life'—a life of morality, a life of caring for others a simple life with a purity of mind. 'The good life is one inspired by love and guided by knowledge.' According to Socrates, 'True knowledge' emerges through dialogue, and systematic questioning and an uncritical claim to knowledge. Unfortunately, 'there are very few Socratic 'philosophers' these days, who know that they lack wisdom. According to Karen Armstrong, 'too many people assume that they also have it, and in matters secular as well as religious appear unwilling even to consider a rival point of view or seriously assess evidence that might qualify their case. The quest for truth has become agnostic and competitive.'

Being Truthful

Practically all the community religions ask us to be truthful or not utter lies. In a court of law, we are asked to speak the truth, the whole truth and nothing but the truth. People normally proclaim that 'I am speaking the truth' thus implying that the other person is being less than truthful. No body has a monopoly over truth. If it is your truth and no body else shares it, then it is questionable if it is really the 'Truth.' So before you claim with certitude to be truthful, ask yourself: Why are you sure? How do you know? Might it not be otherwise?

But what is Truth? In philosophy a statement or proposition to be true, must meet three conditions. The first one is that to know a proposition or statement to be true, one must believe it. But belief alone is insufficient. Before you assert that a statement or a proposition is true, play the critique and critique it. Ask questions in Socratic fashion, so that you are not giving examples of the truth but discovering it for your self as best as you can. In Plato's Dialogue, Socrates wanders around Athens, engaging all and sundry in philosophical debate. Typically he starts with a question, asking, 'What is beauty?', 'What is justice?' What is friendship?', 'What is courage?'

For example some people worship beauty, and others say that 'beauty is in the eye of the beholder. 'Beauty is momentarily in the mind,' it is only a sensory phenomenon. Jean Kerr has this to say: I am tired of all this nonsense about beauty being skin deep. That's deep enough. What do you want—an adorable pancreas? But for John Keats, 'Beauty is truth, truth beauty,'—that is all ye need to know on earth, and all ye need to know.

Socrates would put the questions to people who think they know the answers. In *Laches*, for example, he asks the General Laches and General Nicias, 'What is courage?' Laches answers confidently that it is standing firm in battle. One of the techniques Socrates employs is the **method of counter example**. When Laches and Nicias define, 'courage' as holding fast in battle, Socrates points out that a soldier who stood fast in battle out of reckless and foolish confidence, putting himself and others in danger, could not be described as courageous. Any assertion should be submitted to close critical scrutiny. Socrates enjoyed engaging such people in philosophical debate, and concludes that they really don't know what courage, justice, friendship, truth and so on essentially are. People **think** they know of course.

Finding what is' Truth' has troubled philosophers, but we take things for granted and take umbrage when somebody accuses us of being economic with the truth. Of course most of us do not have the expertise and knowledge or the inclination to be involved in philosophical debates, but we need to note that we view the world and ourselves through the distorted lens of our brains. Freud suggested that the ego 'rejects the unbearable idea, and since then experimental psychologists have been coming out to reveal the multitude of strategies to keep our egos plump and satisfied. By calling on powerful biases in memory and reasoning, the brain can selectively edit and censor the 'Truth' about ourselves and the world making a softer, kinder and altogether more palatable reality.

The brain's other powerful protectorate is reasoning. This might seem odd as our reasoning is supposed to be the compass that guides us towards truth and not away from it. Cordelia Fine in the very aptly entitled book, *A mind of its own—how your brain distorts and deceives*, explains that when our ego is under attack, the best way we can say of our gift of thinking in these circumstances is that we do at least recognise that conclusions cannot be drawn from thin air; we need a bit of evidence to support our case. The problem is that we behave like a smart lawyer searching for evidence to bolster his client's case, rather than a jury searching for the truth. Memory is often the over-zealous secretary who assists in this process by hiding or destroying files that harbour unwanted information. Evidence that supports your case is quickly accepted, and the legal assistants are sent out to find more of the same.

When there are conflicts, the participants claim that their version is the correct one because they believe that they are honest and the other party is not. The problem and the reason why two people can have conflicting recollections of the same event, is that we don't perceive reality: "Our brain makes up the world." says Professor Conway, a cognitive psychologist from Leeds University, "from the colours we see to the experiences we have. The brain is editing the information we take in even before it is laid down as a memory and further editing takes place as the memory is formed." A memory is not a record of reality like a video, it is a rough sample. So when it comes to recollection, the brain makes it up as it goes.

Truth is always via a statement. It has to be a factual one and not a fabricated one. A statement is true if it says what actually the case is. It represents things the way they stand. If things are as the proposition or statement asserts, then the proposition is true. There should be a correspondence between belief and reality. So if you really want to be truthful, don't believe that your version of an event is the correct one, or that only your memory is accurate. Act as a jury would to find the truth as your brain has already worked its wonders and distorted the memory. If you want to go even further, you can remind yourself that even though juries act with the best intentions to try to establish the reality as it was, they merely arrive at a consensus of how things happened, which is not necessarily the truth.

Memory gives us a great deal of information, but not necessarily an accurate picture of events. It can always be relied upon to give us a great amount of detail about a given situation, but there will be holes in it. The mental apparatus is reliable within certain limits.

Moral Compass

The compass is the conscience, the subtle intellect. A compass always points north. Similarly the conscience always points towards the higher realms, the 'Truth.' Some religious groups in the United States really push the point of the 'Moral compass' claiming it is all that is wrong with us. Be it a sage or a criminal, everyone has a conscience. Criminals do not always pay heed to it, because of their overwhelming desire to have certain objects. They are preoccupied by the objects of their desires, be it money, or to get the next fix, or buy alcohol, or to impress their peers. When we are inundated with desires, we forget what is right and wrong, and the conscience gets drowned.

During a discourse of this type, people inevitably point out that conscience is not necessarily the arbiter of right or wrong. Our sense of right and wrong is influenced by our experiences, our education, and our upbringing. Suicide bombers think they are doing the right thing, though innocent people get killed alongside them.

History shows that when a fundamentalist movement is attacked, it invariably becomes more aggressive, bitter and excessive. They become more radical nursing a deep grievance against mainstream culture or foreign cultures. Our ability to harm and kill each other has kept pace with our economic and scientific progress. Fundamentalists take the debate beyond the realm of logic and dispassionate discussion. When one nurses a deep grievance against another culture, it is difficult for such people to keep aggression within safe limits. Karen Armstrong acknowledges the way the minds of fundamentalists work when she says: "In all its forms, fundamentalism is a fiercely reductive faith. In their anxiety and fear, fundamentalists often distort the tradition they are trying to defend. They can, for example, be highly selective of their reading of their scripture."

In democratic countries people have a choice, and they prefer tolerant and humane versions of religion to the imposition of a set of beliefs based on violence, coercion and bigotry. People and governments of such countries have a responsibility to expose the falsehoods, misconceptions and values of extremists.

People are often confused by the word morality, because it conjures up images of having to follow an inflexible set of arbitrary rules. Or, people often restrict themselves to sexual morality only when discussing the concept of morality. Morality is not about condemning others, nor do I think it is something devised by others to keep us in our place. Morality comes out of our natural wish to be 'good.' To be moral is to distinguish between right and wrong, to have an ethically driven code of conduct, and to let judgements be informed by moral conscience.

Morality springs from our belief that there are virtues that are admirable and behaviours / actions that are wrong. It emanates from our natural wish to do good, to be virtuous. Our sense of being virtuous may be small in scale restricted to ourselves and those close to us or it may be big, and universal in nature. Morality is based on the deep understanding and appreciation that others feel happiness and pain just as we do.

When our wants and desires are in conflict with those of our community or society in general, we are acting selfishly. We entertain the belief that we are separate from the rest of the humanity. Such beliefs carry the price of separation from our 'true nature' and the chance of being at peace.

A man or a woman can be good, virtuous and have admirable qualities and be an angel. People can also regress and behave like an animal and be a devil. I have used the word 'animal, and linked it with regression, but some scientists who study animals believe there is a growing evidence that species ranging from mice to primates are governed by moral codes of conduct the same way as humans. Professor Marc Bekoff, an ecologist at University of Colorado, Boulder, believes that morals are hardwired into the brains of all mammals and provide the 'social glue' that allow often aggressive and competitive animals to live together in groups. An imperative code would enhance the chances of their survival.

People who believe in karma tell me that they do not need a moral code because they consider the consequences of their actions. If you believe in cause and effect then you know that you will suffer if you create bad causes and be unhappy. Their reasons for not killing or stealing or being covetous are purely practical. They know that such actions will not improve their lot; therefore they do not indulge in them. They know that they will derive benefit if they are of help to others, so they try to be compassionate and of service to others. Personally I think that with such a philosophy, one can't go wrong. You are living in the moment then, and weighing the consequences of your actions. One can argue that such behaviour is selfish, in that one would thinking of 'self' only, i.e. what is good for me in this situation? But the reality is that it doesn't hurt others and you are being compassionate to yourself and people you are interacting with because you are after good karmas or actions that will do no harm to others only.

I remember witnessing the law of cause and effect in action once. I was travelling with a middle class person in Kenya when he stopped his car to buy some fruit from a roadside seller. The vendor and the buyer haggled for sometime, and the middle class man managed to reduce the price. After buying the fruit, we drove again but after about two miles the man turned back and remarked that he was upset because had reduced the price too much and probably the poor fruiterer had suffered as a consequence. He paid the price first quoted by the fruiterer!

Professor Bekoff presenting his case in a book, *Wild Justice* says, "Just as in humans, the moral nuances of a particular culture or group will be different from another, but they are certainly there. Moral codes are species specific, so they can be difficult to compare with each other or with humans". According to Professor Bekoff, wolves live in high knit social groups that are regulated by strict rules and they have been found to demonstrate fairness. Chimpanzees also demonstrate a sense of justice and those who deviate from the code of conduct of a group are set upon by other members as punishment. There are cases of dolphins helping humans to escapee from sharks, and elephants that have helped antelopes to escape from enclosures.

His findings are controversial, but it is possible that human morality was not formed from scratch but grew out of primate psychology. Human morality incorporates a set of psychological tendencies and capacities such as empathy, reciprocity, a desire for cooperation and harmony in our species.

Human nature is such that we can be wise, understanding and enlightened like Mahatma Gandhi, Martin Luther and Nelson Mandela, or be cruel, callous and maniacs like Hitler, Idi Amin and Saddam Hussein. It is possible that leaders like Robert Mugabe and others start off with the best intentions, until hubris steps in. They stay for too long in unchallenged authority positions or in office. William Pitt understood how power can corrupt when he said, 'unlimited power is apt to corrupt the minds of those who possesses it.'

If we recognise our 'true nature' and are fully aware of our values, we should try to act in accordance with them. We all believe that there are virtues to be admired and actions that are wrong. Many like to uphold the 'Golden Rule' of do as you would like others do to you. The universal values like not to covet some body's property, kill, steal, and not lie are universal values embraced by most religions and wise people. If one is clear about their values, they can be used as a checklist when considering what is right or good and what is not morally right and hence is wrong. We need to think critically and look deeply at our values to discern whether they accord with universal values or do they harm others.

Your values or beliefs should not be constraining, but great liberations as they point you in the right direction. Once the values are clear, they can help us avoid unnecessary suffering on our journey in life. Some times there are conflicting needs and it is hard to see what is right! We often have this dilemma in our lives and ask our selves whether what we have decided is right or wrong. Our values can help in such situations.

Committing ourselves to our values and principles takes us to the realm of intent and action. The said realm is a stage where we endeavour to practise them in our lives. Values should provide a living example. Some of us flaunt them, but if possible, live them and not preach them.

We need to remind ourselves that what we do with intent has real consequences; it has effects that condition our minds for good or ill.

Intellectual discussions and views are important, but in the final analysis, it is what we do with our thoughts that matters. Thoughts normally shape our actions, but we can decide not to follow our thoughts if they are not healthy. Thoughts come and go; there is no restraint or tax on them. There is a line, a gap if you like between naturally occurring thoughts and following those thoughts. In the same vein desires are only desires, it is how we respond to them that matters. But we are responsible for our actions, and will receive the consequences that flow from them.

For Aristotle, a virtue is a habit or a disposition to act. So the cultivation of virtues is the development of moral habits.

Moral Agents

The debate as to whether man is rational or not rational has continued since Aristotle's time. Like animals, human beings move about, and have desires. But the defining mark or essence of man is that he is rational. To be human is to reason, to think by employing practical reason in how to live. Aristotle's view is that it requires the moral agent to determine from the actual facts of an individual case, what is the right course of action in that situation. The person in such a situation should do the sensible thing based on practical wisdom.

To Socrates, truth and virtue were the same. He held that no one ever does evil intentionally, but only by mistaking what is good or right. By thinking for ourselves, in other words by **striving for moral authority**, we reduce unintentional evil, and thus make our souls as good as possible. However in view of what has happened in History since the passing away of Socrates, it is better to qualify this statement and say that there are exceptions to the rule. For some dictators, the only moral authority was themselves.

It is not possible to teach self knowledge, it has to be acquired. Socrates' aim was not to tell the others the truth—he often claimed to be ignorant of it himself—but rather to help them discover it for themselves as best as they could. Socrates invited all comers to join him in inquiry, to search and to discover. This is the process of thinking for oneself, of reasoning out moral issues and dilemmas, not taking hand me down ideas for granted. Plausible answers were not good enough. An individual seeking a meaning and purpose in life, would want to accept the challenge of being ethical for its own sake, and not because it is imposed by the government or laws of the land. A rules based society is by nature a rules bending society.

In Kant's view, human beings are unique in that they are both rational and free. It is this that makes them moral beings. A robot is not free; everything it does is determined by the programmer. If a robot is programmed in such a way that it ends up killing someone the robot can't be held morally responsible. Being a mere robot, it couldn't refuse. Because it has no freedom, and no consciousness, and cannot think, it can't be held morally accountable for what it does.

Human beings by contrast are free; they should know what their moral duty is. That is why they are genuinely moral agents, and why they can be held morally responsible for what they do.

There are studies that show that leaders whose styles are ethical and positive are inspiring. They are sensitive to how other people are feeling, they manage their own feelings and interact smoothly. They can articulate shared values for what they are doing that followers or employees find meaningful or compelling. Such leaders create a positive climate and see a very positive outcome. But a leader who is unethical and coercive has a bad effect on the climate.

Free to Choose

Confucius' first exhortation is that we should find 'the best version of ourselves, showing faithfulness to our ideals as well as forbearance and benevolence to others.'

According to Jean-Paul Sartre, human beings are free, though some would argue that there is no 'absolute freedom'. Even in the United States, 'land of free' people were not 'free' to pursue communism. It is generally accepted that we choose to go along with socially imposed limitations because it works better for us that way. However, this freedom can be an enormous responsibility. So we deceive ourselves, pretending that, like mere physical objects, we are wholly predetermined to be what we are and to behave the way we do. When we deceive ourselves like this, we are not taking responsibility. Anyone who thinks exercising freedom with responsibility has little understanding of just how fascinating, joyful and intriguing everyday life is.

The question of pre-determination has exercised philosophers since the dawn of time. Deciding the extent to which our lives may or not be pre-determined is time consuming. There are certain things scientists claim are passed on in our genes or hard –wired into our brains. Nature versus nurture issue has been in the forefront of Developmental Psychology for a long time. The controversy over ascribing due weight to genetic facts on one hand and environmental ones on the other as factors responsible for the characteristics of an organism has not been resolved. What is sure is that there is only one thing pre-determined about humans and that is—they are humans.

When we perform an action, we do not always consciously think about the future as well the present, and the likely consequences in an uncertain world. We are not always rational in our choices. We are not guided by any principles. So in weighing up the choices, it is advisable to bear in mind not just the immediate costs and benefits, but the future consequences of our present choices as well.

What purpose we have, what our mission statement is, must be freely chosen by us. It is not about rhetoric only, but how we act is up to us also. This responsibility to act is unavoidable. We are at every moment able to break free from our old habits and the roles society or those near to us have handed to us. You can if you are serious about it, choose different values, to find new goals, to forge yourself anew. Simone de Beauvoir (1908-86) says that humans possess a fundamental form of freedom—the freedom to choose, to change, to be other than what is. A person is not determined to be or do anything in particular in the way that a mountain, tree, chair or animal is. We have no essential nature that makes particular forms of behaviour unavoidable. We can choose to live a life new life and adopt new values.

We do not choose a particular family or particular circumstances into which we are born. I might be born into a wealthy family, or I might find myself a slave. These circumstances will inevitably restrict what I am able to do. As Sartre say, I can choose how I **respond** to these circumstances. Even as a slave, I can choose to obey my master's command or disobey and face the consequences.

No belief is absolutely immune to revision in light of experience. Philosophers often distinguish between two kinds of liberty—negative liberty, and positive liberty. Negative liberty is the freedom to pursue your own desires without external hindrance—no one prevents you from doing what you want or forces you to do something else. Positive liberty on the other hand is when you are able to recognise, and lead the kind of life that you consider is the ideal life,—one that a rational person would choose to live.

Defenders of positive liberty argue that negative liberty alone, is compatible to a kind of slavery. Someone who merely follows their appetites in a wholly unconstrained way is not so much free as enslaved by those appetites—like an undisciplined child allowed to spend all day gorging on chocolates and being unruly.

Sartre thinks that the fact that we have the freedom to choose at each moment, to break away from all our old habits and forge ourselves anew is something we are all aware, at some level. Thus Sartre confronts us with unavoidable responsibility to choose and expose the deceptions we perpetuate on ourselves in order to avoid it.

Moral Renewal: For a Personal Code of Conduct

'The only moral absolute is that we should do what will have the best consequences for all those affected by our actions.'

(Peter Singer)

We all need a moral code to live by, a sort of code of conduct. That is why Codes of Conduct exist in most institutions and organisations. Judaism has the Ten Commandments and other religions have laid down their own moral codes. Guru Nanak sees purity of life as the highest object of human endeavour.

Truth surpasses all

But higher still is true living.

Truth is the greatest religion, and truthful conduct is its manifestation.

(Guru Granth Sahib)

Establishing the ultimate truth is fraught with difficulties, but one can always endeavour to be as truthful as possible. In this age, we have become so detached from the idea of morality, of right and wrong, that the subject is treated as a joke. In the past we depended upon religions to awaken and strengthen that nagging inner voice which says, "This feels wrong" or "is this right?" It seems that it is not there in some people or it is suppressed. But if we don't get our morals from religion, we need to source them from somewhere and agree on some values and boundaries for behaviour. It's not always that our behaviour is ethical or we are charitable to others. People do tend to exploit each other. **There have to be no go areas.**

Quite often we say that this is all common sense, but common sense is like cod liver oil, we know it is good for us, but we find ways of avoiding it. We know exercise is good to keep our bodies healthy fit, and trim, but how many of us follow a training regime regularly?

We prefer instant gratification, conspicuous consumption and get rich schemes, the seduction of what Alexander Pope identified as "lures' sordid charm." When it comes to the crunch, we lock our common sense in the attics of our minds, and ignore the nagging of our inner voice. We refuse to ask ourselves the right questions. This is particularly true when we feel that we can make a fast buck. The economist Roger Bootle observes, "the lust after money for nothing has typically led down the road to perdition."

If a tree wants to grow to a great height, the roots have to be very deep first. To resist temptations to get rich overnight or throbbing desire when presented with the prospect of a fast buck, a deep sense of morality is necessary.

Though we may not be conscious of it but 'immoral behaviour does leave a bad taste in the mouth.' In a study carried out by Toronto University in 2009, scientists watched the facial movements of volunteers as they sampled bad-tasting liquids or looked at photographs of dirty lavatories or messy injuries. Their reactions were compared with those that occurred when they were treated unfairly in a laboratory game. Each case produced the same response –a rising of the upper lip and wrinkle of the nose. So we have a sophisticated moral sense of what is right and wrong, but we suppress it or ignore it.

We are not separate from each other, nature and cosmos. The myth of 'me' and others has been responsible for wars, the rape of the planet, and different forms and expressions of human injustice. We are inextricably liked. The action of one affects the other. It is critical that we think in terms of a global family and care for the world we share. The Dalai Lama because of his difficult experiences and upheaval in his own personal life and that of his followers, puts it very elegantly in, *How to Practise—The Way to a Meaningful Life*, when he says: "In a sense, all human beings belong to a single family. We need to embrace the oneness of humanity and show concern for everyone—not just my family or my country or my continent. We must show concern for every being, not just a few who resemble us. Differences of religion, ideology, race, economic system, social system, and government are all secondary."

In advanced countries people feel entitled to happiness in a way that those living in developing countries or those who lived through the two world wars didn't. Many psychologists stress that happiness is not constant joy and absence of pain. It is in fact, an underlying sense of meaningful, honest progress in life and connection with the world. It's living a meaningful life, a fulfilling life.

Spiritual progress depends on a foundation of proper morality.

Evil, Tyranny, Oppression

One who does not terrify others and who has no fear of others;

Should be held as the possessor of divine knowledge, hear O man, says Nanak.

(Guru Granth Sahib)

It is necessary only for the good man to do nothing for evil to triumph.

(Attributed to Burke)

Evil is something which is wicked and immoral. It is normally associated with the forces of the Devil. Discourses on the concept of 'evil' usually produce a distinction between natural disasters or natural evils and evils perpetrated by human beings. Natural disasters are caused by natural events like earth quakes, tidal waves and natural diseases. Evils by human beings include the suffering that results from plundering, murdering and destroying the environment and other people. They are produced by people who put their ideologies in the forefront and consider other human beings to be peripheral.

Sometimes we say that I was obeying orders of some body superior. But we are not helpless automatic machines; we are moral agents capable of making our own free choices, and acting upon them. Critics of free choice often state that if you were a German in the 1930s asserting your right to oppose the regime simply meant dying earlier. Most of the Nazis who didn't obey orders aren't around to tell their tale.

Hannah Arendt (1906-75) author of, *Eichmann in Jerusalem: A report on the banality of Evil*, attended the trial of the war criminal Adolf Eichmann. Arendt thought that Eichmann saw himself simply as doing his duty by following orders. He approached the murder of Jews as just another bureaucratic task assigned to him that he must accomplish to the best of his ability. Her diagnosis is that he had **given up his moral autonomy.** In particular, he did not think or question. He simply obeyed. However, we like to assert that we are living in a civilized society and not in medieval times. This is an age of reason, of Enlightenment. According to Kant, the watchword of Enlightenment is: Have the courage to use your own reason!

It is important to remember that we are not living in Nazi Germany now. We are autonomous and can reason for ourselves. We do not have to deny our moral authority. Universal Declaration of Human Rights charter was drawn up by the United Nations in 1948 after the Second World War to ensure that people do not defer to authority without thinking. The rights include the right to life, liberty, education, and equality before the law; to freedom of movement, religion, association; and to a nationality. The declaration is not legally binding, and the frequent contraventions are monitored by organisations such as Amnesty International.

We think of our short term aspirations or gains only. We start wars for example, and as a consequence of our actions, a great deal of suffering is caused and can be caused. This is wrong use of free will. Free will can be used to benefit humanity and causing suffering as well. Some people even question whether we should be endowed with free will, or whether human beings are rational. As moral agents it is our responsibility to ensure that free will is used for the greater good and not for our selfish ends. Nature has given us the freedom; to ensure that our choices do not harm anyone is our responsibility. We don't have to act on evil thoughts—we can 'disarm evil thoughts.'

"Just as we can't stop birds from flying over our heads, but we can stop them from nesting in our hair, so we can't avoid evil thoughts, but we can stop them from taking root in our heart and giving birth to evil deed."

(Martin Luther. - Germany)

Opposing Oppression/ Tyranny

It is often said that History is written by the winners. However Barrack Obama is right when he says **"Those who stand up for justice are always on the right side of history."**

"The death of one man is a tragedy. The death of millions is a statistic." Stalin's comment made to Churchill at a conference in 1945 now seems bitterly ironic, given how many millions of people died, were dispossessed or imprisoned during his 30 years in power.

Now let us see what Zoya Phan the foremost Burmese human rights activist in exile and author of, *Little Daughter: A Memoir of Survival in Burma and the West*—has to say about her experiences. "My father and mother never had a peaceful life. It was one of sacrifice and struggle. Though they hid it from us, they lived in fear. They showed us how to survive and to be strong." Her father was shot on the veranda of his house by three men in a pickup. He was assassinated because he was a human rights campaigner. His daughter Zoya Phan decided that 'she couldn't let what he believed in die.' All her energy is funnelled outwards—into shaming the world community for supporting the corrupt regime, campaigning for more humanitarian aid and criticising the United Nations for not intervening to stop the ethnic cleansing in eastern Burma. Like every other exile, her dream is to return home to a—Free Burma.

I believe that every right thinking person will agree that every one has the right of free movement in search of truth and in the attainment of moral good, and of justice, and the right to a dignified life.

We can choose to live a 'good' life, a moral life, but there will always be big players on the world stage like Adolf Hitler, and Joseph Stalin, just to name a few, who take over a country and make people's life a hell. Dictators like Saddam Hussein crush the dignity of their subjects under their feet. The nation states and their terrorist allies, then, constitute according to George W. Bush an, "axis of evil." Tyranny gets entrenched and is usually well organised. Some body said very aptly that, 'Tyranny is always better organised than freedom.' We meet 'Godfathers' and lesser tyrants in our every day lives who make the life of families or a community hell.

Injustice corrupts the soul, both of the victim and the one who is unjust. If the oppressed do not do anything, it is doubly wrong then. Usually there are two ways of dealing with oppression: you either fought back or continued being a victim. Some people notably like Mahatma Gandhi, Dalai Lama, and Martin Luther King Jr. believed that fighting back with force is no solution either. Violence begets violence. The original perpetrator of injustice feels victimised and feels justified in responding with violence. Gandhi's three basic values, truth, non violence and self- suffering were combined in his response, which he called *Satyagraha.* The basic idea was to bring an end to injustice by awakening the heart of the wrong doer through love and suffering, his sense of justice.

Martin Luther King was influenced by Mahatma Gandhi's ideas on non violence as a means to change and attain civil rights. He believed that, "At the centre of non-violence stands the principle of love." "Non -violence resistance avoids not only external physical violence but also internal violence of spirit. At the centre of non-violence stands the principle of love. In struggling for human dignity the oppressed people of the world must not allow themselves to become bitter or indulge in hate campaigns. To retaliate with hate and bitterness would do nothing but intensify the hate in the world. Along the way of life, someone must have sense enough and morality enough to cut off the chain of hate. This can be done only by projecting the ethics of love to the centre of our lives."

Just War

When an affair surpasses and goes beyond the region of diplomacy, it is lawful to have recourse to the sword.

(Guru Gobind Singh)

Some religions and people believe that war in some circumstances is just, and that it must be conducted in ways limited by what is right.

Sikhs recognise that in some situations war is necessary. Guru Nanak insisted that tyranny and injustice must be resisted. Guru Gobind Singh the tenth Guru laid five conditions for a justifiable war: (1) It must be action of the last resort, after all other means of settling an issue have been used. (2) The motives must be pure—e.g. free from revenge or enmity. ((3) It must be not be for the purpose of gaining territory, and any gained in conflict must be returned.(4) The soldiers must be committed to a war of righteousness (Dharma Yudh) and therefore must conduct themselves to very high standards—especially in the treatment of non combatants and the defeated. (5) Minimum force must be employed.

St Augustine who became the bishop of Hippo (in Algeria) made some attempt to draw the threads of a Just War theory and the first account appears in Gratian's *Decretum*. Gratian is the author, and his work is the major source of the Roman Catholic canon. The classic form of the theory is that a 'just war' requires:

1. A just cause. There are three components to the just cause: to regain something wrongfully taken, to punish evil, and in defence against planned or actual aggression;
2. A right authority initiating the war;
3. A right intention on the part of those engaged;
4. A proportional use of force, relevant to the issue and not doing more harm than good; and that the war should be undertaken
5. As a last resort;
6. With the purpose.

The Golden Rule

Zigong asked:

Is there any single word that could guide one's entire life?

The master said:

Should it not be 'shu' (reciprocity)? What you do not wish for yourself, do not do to others.

(Confucius)

The Golden Rule appears in different forms in different religions traditions and ethical systems. Sometimes it takes a positive form as in the Christian injunction: Do unto others as you would have them do unto you. (Jesus, Mathew 7:12) Guru Nanak wishes every one in the world well when he says: 'May your Name be exalted and all prosper according to Your Will.'

Confucius offers a vey practical philosophy, containing much sagely advice. He believes that a harmonious and stable society requires among other things a **concern for others.** He thought that 'everything always came back to the importance of treating others with absolute respect.' This was epitomised in the Golden rule which he said his disciples should practise all day and every day. His golden rule is: Never impose on others what you would not choose for yourself." or put slightly differently, 'Do not do to others what you would not want done to you.' It is formulated as a prohibition.

Gandhi used to say that 'all men are brothers because they possess the same *atman* or soul, hence to exploit or injure another is to do violence to oneself.'

The moral of the Golden Rule becomes more plausible when we firmly believe that we should carefully consider when deciding what we should do or not do. It is about Treating Others, as you would like to be treated. Some people argue about what is 'Right' and what is 'Wrong'. According to the Humanists, 'What is right and wrong depends on the effects on people and the consequences for society and the world'. Some would say that it is the intention that counts. According to Immanuel Kant, what matters about an action, so far as its moral worth is concerned is the intention with which it is performed. As rational agents, who want to lead meaningful lives we have certain moral duties, duties forced on us by reason alone. These duties are **categorical** rather than hypothetical.

When you consider the whole of humanity as one family, like the Sikh injunction, 'No one is our enemy, no one is a stranger to us, we have befriended the whole world,' it is difficult to harm others. It would be difficult for a political leader to order the bombing of another country because the inhabitants of the targeted country are not enemies or strangers. They are part of the 'one big family' who may be; require support, understanding and compassion rather than conquest and submission or total annihilation. You have a genuine concern for people irrespective of their origin, background, creed or colour. They are part of the same Soul. Human nature is such that we tend to ignore the pain and suffering of strangers, people you do not know. We try to alleviate the suffering of those who are close to us. If we recognise the whole of humanity as one big family then, it would be difficult to 'impose on others what you would not choose for yourself.'

The Golden Rule should not be taken as a strict prohibition, but as an ethical reminder. As Stephen Laws says in the *Great Philosophers*, "When we weigh up what action to follow, it is easy to forget how deeply our action may affect others, particularly if they are some distance from us. The golden rule reminds us to take a step back and consider our actions from the point of view of those most likely to be affected by them. If a political leader orders the bombing of another country without reflecting on the impact such an action will have on the lives of its inhabitants, we would rightly consider it a badly made decision." Gandhi used to say that 'all men are brothers because they possess the same atman or soul, hence to exploit or injure another is to do violence to one self. The whole universe has welled out from the same Light. (Guru Granth Sahib)

'Never impose on others what you should not choose for yourself 'is an old maxim. Perhaps The Golden Rule becomes more plausible when we think of it as encouraging us to consider carefully what we should do or should not do. Such an analysis and reflection will give meaning and purpose to our life, because we have considered the likely consequences of our actions. We think before we leap. Your life is a 'considered life.'

If we realize that we have made a mistake, or made a bad decision that has perhaps caused suffering to others, then it is imperative that it is acknowledged and ways found to put it right. There is no need to beat oneself up about it; the focus should be on correcting the wrong done. It is the quality of your consciousness at the moment that determines your future actions. The past will perpetuate itself through lack of presence. If you have been unjust, the old pattern can be broken, and the same thoughts and emotions are not acted upon in endless repeat performance.

With the right intention, you will be living in the present rather than dwelling on past mistakes. All the great people have made their share of mistakes, some of them very serious ones indeed, yet they still went on to touch great horizons and were able to offer help and guidance to others. We cannot go back, but we can learn and accept responsibility for our actions. Never give up if you want to succeed in the spiritual life or live a more meaningful life.

Other Sayings

Buddhism

Treat not others in ways that you yourself would find hurtful.

The Buddha, Udana-Varga 5.18

Hinduism

This is the sum of duty: do not do to others what would cause pain if done to you.

Mahabharata 5:1517

Islam

Not one of you truly believes until you wish for others what you wish for yourself

The Prophet Muhammad, Hadith

Jainism

One should treat all creatures in the world as one would like to be treated.

Mahavira, Sutrakritanga

Judaism

That which is hateful to you, do not do to your neighbour

Torah (Hillel's summary)

Sikhism

No one is our enemy; no one is a stranger to use. Indeed, we have befriended the whole humanity.

Guru Granth Sahib, p.1299

Taoism

Regard your neighbour's gain as your own gain and your neighbour's loss as your own loss

Lao Tzu, Tai Shang Kan Ying P'len, 213-218

A Vow for Today

To move to a higher realm, to unravel the beauty within you:

Refrain from engaging in any activity which you know is wrong –anything which harms you physically, mentally, spiritually, socially or emotionally or which harms another human being physically, emotionally and spiritually.

Take the same vow again tomorrow.

Your Values

Rokeach in *The* Nature *of Human Values* (1973) says that values are a "comprehensive set of standards to guide actions, justifications, judgements, and comparison of self and others. Values aid us to serve needs for adjustment, ego defence and self actualization. Values make us tick. Some psychologists contend that a sense of belonging to a community with a set of beliefs and values has positive outcomes in terms of physical health, mental health and longevity.

Values differ from social norms as values are personal and internal. A social norm is a prescription to behave in a certain situation in a specific way. For example, in the United Kingdom, we used to stand up when the national anthem was played in public places but not when we heard it over the radio or saw it on television at home.

Why have any values? What purposes do they serve?

- Values can be seen as standards that guide ongoing activities.
- Values give expression to human need.
- Values are multifaceted standards that guide our conduct in a variety of ways.
- Values are central to the study of comparisons. We employ them to ascertain whether we are as moral and competent as others.

Some believe that principles and values are subjective. Graham Leonard (former Bishop of London) in a lecture about the 'tyranny of subjectivism' argued that: "Subjectivism is based on the belief that principles and values are in essence no more than statements about the likes and dislikes, desires and aversions of those who hold them. From this it follows that there is no possibility of any resolution of disagreements about questions of principles and value or even of politics. There can be no more on the part of the subjectivist, than the restatement of what he considers to be self-evident truths and he is impervious to the arguments or criticisms of those who seek to challenge him."

There is a problem here with attempting to say that subjectivism is something we can avoid. Since we only communicate through the use of language and language is fluid and has no absolutes, almost every thing we say is in some sense subjective. Even if we claim that we have definitive answers, we can only express these by using language concepts. Due to the nature of language, it is not possible to establish anything definitively—no matter how we construct our arguments.

Rokeach contends that a value refers to a mode of conduct or end state. A value represents a specific preference. A person prefers a mode (instrumental) or end state (terminal value) not only when he or she compares it with the opposite, but also when comparing with other values within his or her value system. The person prefers a particular mode or end state to other modes or end states that are lower down in his or her value hierarchy. Thus people who value contentment as a terminal value, (end state) can have cessation of craving as their instrumental value (mode).

That is why the manner in which a person copes with his problems is the most revealing thing about him. In *Opinions and Personality,* Smith, Bruner and White state that, - "The solutions to his problems are conserved in the form of values: ways of looking at and evaluating himself, the people about him, and the world around him." For example, our attitude or response to difficult circumstances such as terminal illness will normally be shaped by on one of our central values.

Any small activity that is done within the framework of your values will bring a profound sense of satisfaction, joy, and depth of meaning to your life. The direct result is that you value yourself much more. Values add spice to your life. VALUES are maps, principles are territory. Correct maps will infinitely impact our personal and interpersonal effectiveness far more than any effort expended on changing our attitudes and behaviours. According to Yu Dan, 'people who have built up a clear and lucid system of values are able to transform the pressures of our society into a flexible strength that allows them to bounce back.'(*Confucius from the Heart—Ancient wisdom for Today's World*)

If your spirit has taken its stand, and you have adhered to moral values, become more calm and relaxed, then you can safely say that you have lived a truly meaningful life up this point in time.

Identify your Values

Only by building up a system of values for the heart, can we change pressure into flexibility and spring back.

(Yu Dan—Confucius from the Heart)

Many of us end up giving lip service to certain values such as I want to be 'more compassionate,' or 'I want a balanced life,' but actually living in a totally different way. It's hard to unearth your values. It's what you like, what moves you and what you are like. That is why the social psychologists - Smith et al contend that, "Among the most revealing procedure used in our exploration on Personal Values and Religious Sentiments, began with a question on: **What things really matter to you most in life? - and moved widely over the philosophy of life."** You can see the disconnect between what your real values are and what you imagine them to be if you contemplate on life, your philosophy and what rally matters to you most in life.

When you have a messy dilemma with more than one option, and you find yourself flummoxed as to what the right solution is for you, consider the short term and long term consequences of your actions, their upsides and downsides. You can't do much about the past but you can change the course of the future, within reason, by how you make decisions today or **now**. You can say to yourself, "I will make decisions that match how I want to live." It will give you a framework and obviously you want to gather the right data before making a decision. You can move from making guilt driven decisions to value driven decisions which hopefully you will not regret or make you cry later.

As mentioned above, Gandhi's three basic values were: truth, nonviolence and self suffering. In fact he believed that God Is Truth, Truth Is God. His civil disobedience was based on these values. He did not only preach these values, but provided a living example.

When ever you feel a sense of something mattering, then you are touching on something that is a 'value' for you. A value therefore is something to which you are drawn naturally. It is something you consciously decide because it has merits or even because it is logical. Values incorporate one's principles or standards, one's judgement of what is valuable or important in life.

May be it's time to think hard about your values now and answer the three questions that will help you to see if you are a living example also:

- What are your values?
- Do they help or hinder you to lead a good life?
- Do you live by them or just pay lip service to them?

One can infer much about a person by letting him tell what he likes, what moves him and what he is like. That is why the social psychologists - Smith et al contend that the 'Personality of a person can best be studied by understanding a man's values and philosophy.

(For a deeper discussion on Values, please see, *Achieving Inner Peace*)

Footnotes

Karma: Sanskrit, Pali—'action, 'deed'. ' In Asian religions, it is the sum of a person's own actions in this and previous states of existence. According to karma theory, every action has a consequence which will come to fruition in either this or future life; thus morally good acts will have positive consequences, whereas bad acts will produce negative results. Gautama Buddha summed it up by saying, 'whatever deeds (karma) they do —good or evil—of such they will be the heirs. And wherever the beings spring into existence, their deeds will ripen; and wherever their deeds ripen , there they will earn the fruits of their deeds, be it in this life, or be it in the next life, or be it in any other future life...' According to Sikhism, repentance, meditation, and Grace of God can put an end to the vicious cycle of Karma. To invoke God 's Grace, a person must do meditation and must perform good karmas. A person who does not perform any prayers and who continuously and deliberately indulges in bad actions cannot get God 's Grace and thus must suffer for his bad actions.

Conclusion

Humankind has made great strides in improving our knowledge base; science has opened our lives to greater opportunities. Up to a measure, we are able to mould and modify practically most things for our convenience. As a matter of fact, science has replaced mythologies as a framework for understanding the world, as it is supposed to bring with it its enquiring, questioning, experimentation, and open attitudes. Leading scientists are like high priests in that they have knowledge not available to most. Thus science has become a sort of mythology itself. Mythology is the study of myths. A myth according to my dictionary is a traditional story concerning the early history of people or explaining a natural or social phenomenon, and typically involving supernatural beings or events.

Science had promoted the notion of individual liberty, in that it supposedly allows the individual to gain and apply knowledge and enjoy different pleasures and attractions. However some discoveries are bewildering to scientists, and utterly beyond the grasp of the layperson. Lately it has become disturbingly clear that not only science was unable to provide us with definitive proof, but findings by one scientist are immediately challenged by another. Some bold, imaginative guesses that could never be properly verified are no more reliable than any other 'belief.' Human beings never achieved perfect knowledge because anything we know at any given time is invariably revised later.

Karen Armstrong argues that, 'religious leaders often spend more time enforcing doctrinal conformity than devising spiritual exercise that will make the official 'beliefs' a living reality in the daily lives of the faithful. Instead of using scripture to help people to move forward and embrace new attitudes, people quote ancient scriptural texts to prevent any such progress.'

We live in spiritual confusion because of the above factors and our materialist culture. People still say, 'Oh I feel so empty inside, or my life is meaningless.' We follow the advice churned out by remote authorities like pop psychologists, doctors and the 'welfare industry.' Eager to feel more fulfilled or less agonized about ourselves, we go for that 'expensive break' or follow the 'nine steps to eternal happiness,' drink the potion, follow that regime, and read the book by the 'know it all author,' but still the emptiness does not go. We get more and more bewildered. That is not surprising, because we listen to others, but do not dive deep within ourselves. Confucius has rightly pointed out that, 'If one learns from others but does not think, one will be bewildered.' I hope this 'work' helps you to dive deep within for, 'Pearls do not lie on the sea shore. If you desire one, you must dive for it.' 'Desire' can be transformed into the driving force of your life leading you to a better understanding of your real purpose in this world and to make your life a little more meaningful.

Religion has a lot to offer, but it has to be practised. The truth of the scripture is acquired by practical action. One cannot drive a car simply by reading the manual or study the Highway Code. You need to learn to swim to cross a river or go to the other end of the pool. A novice, who has not learnt and practised swimming, will sink to the bottom of a pool or river. You have to translate the doctrines into ethical action. A person on a spiritual path has to contemplate the teaching and not just listen to what the scripture or expositors say. Guru Nanak asks a disciple to use his intelligence to examine the commodity before trading in it. Religious life is an experience. One has to adopt the discipline of truth, and by mounting the ladder of spirituality go higher and higher. Some people 'who practise it constantly discover a transcendent dimension of life, that is not simply an external reality 'out there' but is identical with the deepest level of their being.'

After all as Nick Williams says, 'within us we hold our spirit, our true holy nature, an aspect of the divine whole, a wonder within our being. Though for many of us our true self is an intimate stranger, we live with it, even if we don't know it well.' Creating our purpose and meaning from the inside out, our essence calls us to start from a new place, from our being. Our spirit calls us to the present moment, to the creation of a meaningful life. Each of us is entitled to and capable of having a life with a purpose and meaning.

A tree is known from the fruits it bears, so a person's religion is known from the deeds that they perform. Robes, symbols, forms, rites, rituals, ceremonies that do not lead to righteous deeds will not take us far on the path of spiritual progress.

When you see life as meaningless, you view yourself as powerless, view the people around you as up to no good, as selfish, and you create painful experiences. Control of your time / life is crucial. When you see life as having a meaning, with a purpose, a creative spirit, your life becomes loving and compassionate. You look at your life as unique, and beautiful. You are then like Confucius' enlightened person, 'The superior person is quiet and calm, waiting patiently for heaven's appointments. The inferior person treads a dangerous way…"

Lessons from Death

The birth and leaving of close ones sometimes compel us to in some profound way to adjust our compass bearings—which way should we be facing.

(From-*The Secret Power of Light)*

The death of a close relative or friend may be the most painful experience of all; but it's important to focus on learning when there is pain. To do this, we need to ask, 'What has the death taught me? How can I change my thinking and behaviour and not be a stick-in the-mud? How can I use this knowledge to improve the quality and purpose of my life and of those around me? Seeing things in this light, it is possible that death can have a positive and life enhancing value. You can derive meanings from death. Thus we can use death which is inevitable to live our lives in a more meaningful way.

Now imagine you are in your final moments, you are tranquil, and your thoughts are clear. Think back about the course of your life. What brought you the greatest satisfaction? What were your biggest disappointments and regrets? What were your strengths? Do you feel you did your best? Were you clear about the purpose and meaning of your life? Did you make a contribution to others? How would you evaluate your life as a whole?

Most likely you can get in touch with a number of regrets, bad decisions, and ways you wasted your precious time. But fortunately it's not the end of your life. You have the time to correct some of the regrets and make changes in your life. It gives you an opportunity to change your life for the better, to make important changes, and put your energy into the things that matter most. After the fear of death is reduced, we can move forward and learn from past experiences. If you have made mistakes, have regrets; make sure that it doesn't happen again. Use the reflection on past experiences positively to try to carry on and live your life as meaningfully as possible.

Some suggestions to make your life more meaningful:

- *You are what you think.* You can decide what you want to do before your departure from this world.
- How would you like to be remembered? Now think about your eulogy.
- Everyone can be significant in some way. How can you change your life for the better?

Michael Angelo said that inside every block of stone dwells a beautiful statue. We all have a beauty within us, but we ignore it, and concentrate on outer attractions, and our desires. Some of us set out to make sense of the world, but get distracted by external influences and lose sight of the purpose and meaning we were searching. 'Our life is gold, in an untidy bag.' We do no have time to unravel the beauty within, or to tap our inner resources. Our goal normally is external enrichment, and inner happiness tends to elude us. The endeavour should be to achieve an amalgam of external enrichment and spiritual excellence. You are then guided by higher values and beliefs because you know that your life has a purpose and a meaning.

Ultimately we have an essential purpose to make our lives more meaningful, to be more conscious of our personal responsibilities and social duties. We can pursue our profession, have a family, enjoy life, but at the same time through all this, life will have a focus. You are conscious of your mission in life, your *raison d'être.* You will not live a mechanical life, but will have a higher mission, a higher goal.

Our willingness to act on our moral values, combined with a deep desire to improve and grow opens us up to our spiritual enhancement if not greatness. There may be sacrifices involved, a major change in life style, but if there is a deep desire to build for ourselves a truly worthwhile life, to live peacefully, the goal can be achieved. It will be a life in which you have no regrets when the journey of life comes to an end.

When death comes, you accept it, knowing fully that you have left this world a slightly better place. You are ready for the next life, or to meet the Supreme Being. You 'found the best version of yourself' and the real meaning and purpose of your life. You showed faithfulness to your ideals, and values as well as forbearance and benevolence to others. When the day of death comes, there is no fear to die, for you have led a 'good life,' a considered life, which kept the meaning and purpose of your life in the forefront.

You might have held the view that you are better off as you are and don't really have the deep desire to find peace and meaning in your life. You were satisfied with your present life style. You were not willing to give up certain things which you enjoyed. You wanted to remain in your comfort zone. I hope that this 'work' has gone some way to raising your awareness and sensitivity to life.

References

1. Arberry, A.J., (Translated by) *Mystical Poems Of Rumi, First Selection, Poems 1-200*, (Chicago, London, 1968).
2. Armstrong, K., *The Case for God, What Religion Really Means*. (London, 2009).
3. Bhaktivedanta, A.C., *Krisna, The Supreme personality of Godhead,* (Los Angeles 1970).
4. Braybrook, M, (ed.), *The Bridge of Stars, 365 Prayers, Blessings and Meditations from Around the World,* (London, 2001).
5. Bowker, J., *Beliefs That Changed The World, The History And Ideas Of The Great Religions* (London, 2007).
6. Bowker, J., *The Meanings of Death* (Cambridge, 1996).
7. Bowker, J., (Ed.), *The Oxford Dictionary Of World Religions,* (Oxford, 2003).
8. Braybrook , M, (Ed.), *The Bridge Of Stars, 365 Prayers, Blessings And Meditations From Around The World,* (London 2001).
9. Bullock. A., Trombley, S, (eds.), The *New Fontana Dictionary of Modern Thought,* (London, 1999).
10. Cook D., *The Moral Maze, A Way of Exploring Christian Ethics.* (London, 1992).

11. Lama, L. Narrated by Goleman D., *Destructive Emotions, And How We Can Overcome Them*, (London, 2004).

12. Dan Y., *Confucius from the Heart, Ancient Wisdom For Today's World*. (London 2009).

13. Dilgeer, H. S., *The Sikh Culture* .(Sikh Centre- Belgium, 1992).

14. Enrique, C. A. (ed.), *Descartes, Key Philosophical Writings*. (Hertfordshire 1999).

15. Fine, C., *A Mind Of Its Own, How Your Mind Distorts And Deceives*, (Cambridge, 2006).

16. Frankl , V. E., *Man's Search for Ultimate Meaning,* (New York, 2000).

17. Fry, C., *Life Before Death*. (London, Sydney, 2007).

18. Gill. D., et al., *World Religions, The Essential Reference Guide to the World's Major Faiths*, (2003, London).

19. Grayling, A.C., *What Is Good, The Search For The Best Way To Live*, (London, 2004).

20. H.H Dalai L. Translated and (Ed.), Hopkins, J., *How to Practise, The Way To A Meaningful Life (*2008).

21. H. H. Lama, D. & Cutter, H. C. (MD.), *The Art Of Happiness At Work* (London, 2003).

22. Holden, M., *Boundless Love, Transforming Your Life With Grace And Inspiration*. (London, Sydney, 2002).

23. Kapoor, S.S., *Sikhism, An Introduction (*Amritsar, 2007).

24. Kohli, S. S., *The Sikh Philosophy* (Amritsar, 2002).

25. Law, S., *The Great Philosophers, The Lives and Ideas of History's Greatest Thinkers* (London, 2007).

26. Lee, D., (translated by), *Plato, The Republic*, (London,2007).

27. Lowne, C., (compiled by), *Speeches That Changed The World,* (London, 2005).

28. Morgan, D., *Sitting Buddha, Zen meditation For Everyone,* (Carr shield, Hexham, 2004).

29. Patel, M., *The Secret Power of Light*, (2000).

30. Picard, M., *This is Not A Book, Adventures In Popular Philosophy*, (London, 2007).

31. Rokeach, M., *The Nature of human Values,* (New York, 1977).

32. Rinpoche, S., *The Tibetan Book Of Living And Dying,* (London, Sydney, 2008).

33. Rolland P., *Reincarnation, Remarkable Stories Of People Who Recall Past Lives,* (London 2009).

34. Ross, E.K., *Death and Dying,* (New York 2003).

35. Row, J., *Profile Of The Perfect Person, Based On The Bhagawad Gita Chapter 2*, (Mumbai 2007).

36. Sarwar, G., *Islam, Beliefs And Teachings,* (London 2006).

37. Stokes, P., *Philosophy, The Great Thinkers,* (London, 2008).

38. Tolle, E., *The Power Of Now, A Guide To Spiritual Enlightenment*, (London, 2009).

39. Williams N., *The Work We born To Do, Find The Work You Love, Love The Work You Do,* (London, 2007).

Index